TOTAL NONSTOP AGONY

TOTAL NONSTOP AGONY

THE RISE AND FALL OF TNA

VINCE RUSSO

ECW

Published by ECW Press
665 Gerrard Street East
Toronto, Ontario, Canada M4M 1Y2
416-694-3348 / info@ecwpress.com

CERTIFIED CANADIAN PUBLISHER

Editor for the Press: Michael Holmes
Copy editor: Rachel Ironstone
Cover design: Jessica Albert
Photo of Eric Bischoff © WWE / Courtesy Everett Collection
Photo of Hulk Hogan by Dave Moss via
Wikimedia Commons, CC BY-SA 2.0
Still image of Vince Russo from WCW broadcast footage

LIBRARY AND ARCHIVES CANADA CATALOGUING IN PUBLICATION

Title: Total nonstop agony : the rise and fall of TNA / Vince Russo.

Names: Russo, Vince, 1961- author.

Identifiers: Canadiana (print) 20260121568 | Canadiana (ebook) 20260121576

ISBN 978-1-77041-846-2 (softcover)
ISBN 978-1-77852-559-9 (ePub)
ISBN 978-1-77852-560-5 (PDF)

Subjects: LCSH: Russo, Vince, 1961- | LCSH: Total Nonstop Action Wrestling. | LCSH: Wrestling promoters—United States—Biography. | LCGFT: Autobiographies.

Classification: LCC GV1196.R87 A3 2026 | DDC 796.812092—dc23

PRINTED AND BOUND IN CANADA

PRINTING: FRIESENS 5 4 3 2 1

This book is dedicated to my two sweet little angels, Amelia and Emery. I hope that when they are old enough they can read their "PaPa's" words and know what kind of a man he was and what he represented and stood for. But, most importantly, I want them to always know—he loved his FAMILY more than anything in the world and nothing else was even a close second.

AUTHOR'S NOTE: The memoir you are about to read is the third and final installment of a trilogy. It is recommended that you read the first two books, *Forgiven* and *Rope Opera*, to fully understand the journey. No, I am not telling you that in an attempt to sell you two more books, I'm simply stating that if you want a complete and full understanding of my story, it would be of benefit to read all three volumes.

CONTENTS

1 "HOGAN, YOU BIG, BALD SON-OF-A-BITCH!"

"Vince, you've got to start hot. You've got to start with controversy. Begin with something that is immediately going to commit and invest the reader."

As I sit down at this keyboard, a place where I've lived too many hours to count, I can hear the words of my editor, Michael Holmes, as if he were sitting next to me. It's all about starting hot. Whether it is a book or the highest-rated televised wrestling show in history, the objective is to hook your audience immediately.

OK . . . here we go.

"HOGAN, YOU BIG, BALD SON-OF-A-BITCH!"

That should do it.

The eight words that have defined me to thousands—if not millions—over the last 25 years, The eight words of a "wrestling promo" that, to this very minute, the majority believe was a "shoot" (real), no matter how many times I tell them that both Hulk Hogan and Eric Bischoff were in on it.

And they were.

I'm almost 65 years old, why in the name of all that is sane would I lie about anything wrestling-related that took place over 25 years ago—a quarter of a *century* to be more specific. Why? What would be my motivation? What would I possibly gain from it?

Since me making this story up would make no sense to anybody, I'm constantly asking myself, "Do they believe it was a shoot because they want to believe it was a shoot?" Do they want to believe that a brash, arrogant New Yawker finally put Hulk Hogan, the greatest, most self-serving wrestling politician of all time, in his place?

Or, do they believe it was a shoot because Hulk and Bischoff have stated on the record that they knew nothing about the promo I cut that infamous July night on *WCW Bash at the Beach*?

Well, they were *partially* right . . . I guess.

For me, as an on-screen performer, it was always about being in the moment. I never wrote out a script for myself—who could perform that way? Memorizing words from a piece of paper comes across exactly as that—rehearsed. When I had to cut a promo (in-ring dialogue), I always put myself in the moment. What was happening to my character at that point in time? Everything I ever wrote or acted out in professional wrestling came from the mindset, "if this were real . . ."

And, at that time, that promo was real. That's how I felt at that very moment. That night, I had reached my limit; I had finally had enough with pro wrestling and all the politics and bullshit that went along with it. I was done with it. I just wanted to go home and be with my wife and kids. However, while real emotion was fueling my words, my character had to cut that promo in order to make sense of a match being made. I had to connect the dots to make the audience believe that the main event between Jeff Jarrett and Booker T was real, coming out of the series of events that had taken place prior.

And the audience bought it—all of it. They engulfed the hook and took every word spoken from my mouth as gospel. That's why no matter how many times people question me about it, I will never call Bischoff and Hogan liars for saying I "went into business for myself." They knew I was going to cut a "scathing" promo on Hulk because I told them prior, but truth I didn't tell them *exactly* what I was going to say simply because I didn't know. I never knew what I was going to say in the ring in advance. So the question is: Was my promo so convincing that even Eric and Hulk believed its authenticity? Well, maybe . . . but maybe not.

I'm of the opinion that the heat with Hogan came from those who watched it believing it was factual, thus believing that I got over on the Hulkster. I'm fairly confident that's what triggered the defamation lawsuit he filed against me. Millions of people actually believed that Vince Russo put Hulk Hogan in his place, and that was a tough blow to Hulk's ego. And as far as Bischoff goes, he was just going to back whatever his cash cow had to say—true, false, or indifferent.

But those eight words from that fictitious promo have stayed with me for most of my adult and senior life. For many, they define my entire career. Mainly by my adversaries who want to believe that Vince Russo, the *real* Vince Russo, was and still is really that guy they saw on TV. The majority want to believe that simply because many people just hate New Yorkers. That is a bias that I dealt with throughout my entire wrestling career. Don't believe me? Just ask Jim Cornette.

New Yorkers represent the *truth*. We are going to tell you what we think and how we feel whether you want to hear it or not. Unfortunately, that doesn't work in a wrestling bubble made up of liars, cheaters, con men, snake oil salesmen, and carnie clowns. *Nobody* wants to hear the truth in professional wrestling. It is against everything they believe . . . You know: "THE WORK."

I don't know if you're ready to hear this yet, but professional wrestling is a lie. *It's all a lie.* It's an industry trying to convince you that everything you're seeing is real . . . when, in fact, it's not (or at least that's the way it used to be). That deception causes everybody who is involved to always be "working," or not telling the truth. Unfortunately, that tomfoolery takes place not only in front of the camera, but also behind it.

Being honest in the wrestling business killed me. It kills me to this day. I'm blackballed from a business I spent 34 years in simply because I've stayed true to myself. From the very first day I stepped into Johnny Rodz's wrestling school to learn the tricks of the trade, I've always been a hundred-percent honest. I've never had an agenda, sold out, kissed ass, or been a tool for anybody. My New York pride and integrity always superseded trying to get ahead.

But, regardless, my critics love calling me a liar. They claim I lie about everything. Can you imagine? What would I possible lie about pertaining to the wrestling business, let alone two and a half decades after the fact?

But liars, true liars, they want to believe everybody is lying to justify their own lies.

Man, every day I worked, when I woke up, I had to look at my wife, Amy, and my three kids, Will, VJ, and Annie. I always wanted them to be so proud of me and what I stood for. I wanted them to learn honor from me, pride, dignity, respect, integrity, and honesty. I wanted them to know that their husband and father was REAL—No Bullshit REAL.

And being real has got me right here, right now—on the outside, looking in—and I wouldn't want it any other way.

2 WHY THE !@#$%^& AM I DOING THIS?

OK, Michael, I opened hot. Now the real question: Why the !@#$%^& am I doing this?

Honestly . . . I'm not sure. So let me ask myself again: Why the !@#$%^& AM I DOING THIS?

I guess the answer may lie with my wife; Amy has been telling me this since 1983: "Vin, you do this to yourself."

And she's right; I *do* do this to myself. It's nobody else's fault. I'm a glutton, a hundred-percent. I hate everything about having to write this book. Did I say *having*? As if somebody were making me, or forcing me to write? No. I planted the seed in Michael's head. While on a phone call with him attempting to get a friend's book published, I blurted out, "So . . . when are we going to write the third installment?" Wait a minute . . . *we*? What *we*? Michael wasn't going to be sitting behind my screen, on my keyboard, agonizing over every word written as I revisit a place that I loathe and never want to go back to. NO! It's going to be me doing that. Am I insane?

Maybe.

But, in fairness, at this point in my life, my brain truly doesn't function the same way it did even 10 years ago. I blame it on the recurring concussions I suffered in the ring. You ever listen to one of my podcasts? I should have been featured on the Beatles' infamous *Yesterday and Today* album cover—butchery's what I do to the English language. Some even say I make legendary comedian Norm Crosby look like a thespian! I butcher so many names that sometimes even my co-host Jeff Lane doesn't know who I'm talking about. And what makes it even worse is—I don't care. As a matter of fact, I've convinced myself that it's an honor if I filet your name. But the good news—even though I'm not of the mental prowess I once was—is I don't think I've lost my sanity . . . yet.

So then . . . why?

WHY?

I've got to really dig here to find the truth, and the fun is that I'm going to do it right now, right here with you. The first obvious reason would be the money. At this point in my life, a few years away from at least *semi*-retirement, I'm looking to sock away as much capital as possible. The ultimate dream is to buy a cabin in the mountains and just disappear on my 65th birthday. That . . . is going to take money.

I have to laugh every time I'm on Twitch, hustling for a buck, when some assclown comes on and tells me how many millions I have in the bank according to "some website." Website? Millions? WHERE? Where are these millions? I think many forget that I was a lowly writer/producer. I didn't make *WrestleMania* money—I didn't even make a fraction of that. I made what writers make, and though I'm not complaining, it definitely wasn't enough to retire on when I walked away from the business 13 years ago. No, man, I had to keep hustling, keep grinding, much like I continue to do today.

Unfortunately, writing this book isn't going to make me rich. It's going to be a satisfying accomplishment, but it ain't buying no cabin in no woods where I no longer have to work and can just look at the elk all day.

So we can rule out money.

I'm about to make a confession—and if you know me, you already know this. I am a workaholic. It's a disease. It started in college and has only gotten worse over the years. I learned work ethic at Indiana State. There was a time when I was *all* of the following at once:

1. editor of student newspaper
2. vice president of Sigma Tau Gamma
3. PR director of the student union board

4. projectionist for Dr. Blevins's film class
5. clerk at Movies to Go
6. salesman at Allied Sporting Goods

That's where it all started, and it has continued for over 40 years. I can't stop. I want to stop . . . but I can't. Every few months, when I find myself burning out, I will always make an effort to "clear my plate." Then, within the next few weeks, I'll start filling that plate all over again, until I have more on it than I did before I tried cutting back.

"Vin, you do this to yourself."

She's right—I do. But I can't help it. It's just this drive that lives deep within me. If I'm not working, I feel guilty, as if I should be. I can't relax; I can't even sit. I always have to be moving, always. My mind, my fingers, my voice, always working . . . always producing . . . always creating. There's never a good night's sleep. I'm always up, even when I don't want to be. I go as far as getting pissed at myself for not being able to sleep. This can't be healthy, but this is my life.

So, subconsciously, that's why I brought it up to Michael. I hated the idea of doing it, while at the same time reveling in all the involved work that was ahead. I know the memories are going to hurt. They've always hurt. The wrestling business has left physical, mental, and emotional scars on me that will never heal—never. But yet . . . here I am.

You always hear that something can be a blessing and a curse at the same time—that's the professional wrestling business to me. A blessing because I've been able to make a living from it for some 34 years now, and a curse because I hate it—I loathe it to the core. It has done damage to me, it has hurt me, and it has changed me.

Come along for this ride and you are going to see that firsthand. That is the commitment that I've made.

Everything will be left on the pages of this book.

3 STREAM OF CONSCIOUSNESS

So now that I've made a commitment to you, you must make one to me—stay with me.

This book is going to be written in a "stream of consciousness" style. What that means is that I'm going to write about things as they come to me. Now, the words might not fit exactly where they should, but if I don't put my thoughts in the here and now . . . they will be forgotten in seconds.

This is something that just comes with age. However, in my case, there's probably a bit more to it.

Since the writing of my last book, my mother passed away from dementia. Over the years, and right before my very eyes, I witnessed my beloved "Fruity" (as in crazy) slowly fade away. It was painful. A strong Italian woman, so set in her ways and as stubborn as they come, became almost childlike. In her later years, she didn't know where I lived, that I was married, nor that she had grandchildren. She would constantly ask me the simplest of questions, much like my granddaughter Amelia did on her first day of kindergarten.

The end came fast and rapidly for Fruity. It got to the point where it was too difficult for my dad to wait on her hand and foot every day; he, himself, was getting up there in age too. At that point, Dad put Mom in a nursing home, where she declined daily until she succumbed to her disease.

I bring this up knowing that dementia is hereditary. Matter of fact, there is a test I can take to see if I'm going to be cursed with it in my later years. My older sister, Debbie, took the test and came up positive. Me? I refuse to because I already know the results.

At this point in my life, things just don't come to me as quickly as they used to, and if something comes to my mind, I need to blurt it out immediately or else I'll forget. Just ask Jeff Lane, who I am constantly interrupting on our shows. Not because my thoughts are more important than his or that I'm rude, but simply because I will immediately forget if things from my brain don't leave my mouth in under three seconds.

Now, marry that to the many, and I mean MANY concussions I experience while at WCW, and I think it's fair to say that I'm just not the same guy I used to be.

STREAM OF CONSCIOUSNESS

Man, I cannot deal with death . . . I just cannot deal with loss. I think this may have come when I was very young and my grandfather's mother passed away. I remember, as a child, going to the funeral and seeing Grandma Saverino laid out in her casket. I don't think I was even five years old yet, but her powder blue dress and matching shoes still vividly live in my 64-year-old mind.

I put the death of my mother way back in the top shelf of my closet. I've never dealt with it because I just can't . . . it's too painful. I can't deal with hurt. I've never been able to deal with hurt . . . real hurt. My dad is 94 years old as I write this. I talk to him on the phone every single day, never missing even one. I can't imagine life without him, and I think about that. I need to prepare myself for the inevitable, which can come at any point after 94. It was literally just a few weeks ago that he had a heart attack . . . I'm still struggling with that as I write this.

Death, or the fear of death, is something that has always been with me. And, quite honestly, I am ashamed to say that because as a Christian I do believe in Jesus Christ with all my heart and soul. I do believe that we are living in hell on earth and our paradise is waiting for us in a place much different from here . . . but . . . I've never been able to shake the fear of the unknown.

How the hell did I just go down that path? I know what you want, so let's get back to rasslin'.

4 WHERE *ROPE OPERA* LEFT OFF

I was met with quite the surprise yesterday when I skimmed through my second book, *Rope Opera: How WCW Killed Vince Russo*, in order to see where to pick this story up. I didn't think I covered TNA at all in my last book, but I did . . . extensively. So, my first thought was, "Oh my God, is there enough of the story left to write an entire book about?" You'll be glad to know that the answer is YES.

When I finished writing *Rope Opera*, I left you at the point where Hulk Hogan and Eric Bischoff had just arrived in the company. As a matter of fact, the book ends as I just started my working relationship with Easy E. Now, it's safe to say, at that point in time I had no way of knowing that it was the beginning of the end of my almost-10-year career at TNA. But . . . it was.

Wait a minute, saying "I had no way of knowing it would be the beginning of the end" is absolute bullshit. Of course I knew. Maybe subconsciously I knew I was going to do my part to just get along for the sake of getting along, but I'm talking about Eric Bischoff here.

Now, let's make one thing clear from the jump (I don't know why I love that phrase), I'm not going to bury Eric here, matter of fact I have no intention of burying anyone in this book. At this stage in my life, there's just no point to it. I'm a true believer that everything happening in your life is happening for a reason. If God is completely in control, then he authored your book. Every day, minute, second was determined before you were spit out of the womb, and once you fully accept that you will be far more understanding of your circumstances.

But if you're asking me if at any point I ever liked Eric Bischoff—the answer is an immediate NO. I didn't like him the day that I met him, and I certainly don't like him 25 years later. And guess what? Eric's sentiments towards me are a hundred-percent identical. I can remember my very first phone conversation with Eric, the very first time I met him in our infamous "clandestine" meeting at the now-defunct Hops in Atlanta. From that very first impression, I thought he was the most arrogant, smug, and egotistical, full-of-himself person I had ever met in my entire life, and remember I was connected at the hip to Vince McMahon for the better part of three years.

Was it a work? Was Eric playing a character? Truth be told, I still don't know. Eric recently celebrated his wedding anniversary online with pictures of himself and his lovely wife, Loree. And what did I see? I saw a loving husband. I also got to witness how Eric was with his son, Garett, and that appeared as solid as a father-son relationship could be. So what I'm saying is I highly doubt the up close and personal Eric Bischoff is . . . well . . . a prick. But to me . . . he was, is, and always will be.

But the older I get, the more I understand the psyche of "lifers" in the "wrestling bubble," I realize that it's *all shtick*. People like Eric and James E. (Cornette) have just never moved on from portraying the characters they were on TV. Matter of fact, in many ways, they have literally become them. And you know what—if that makes them happy . . . great. My wrestling persona died the day I left the microphone behind in the ring. Today, who I am . . . *for real* . . . is who you get.

5 MY FIRST MEETING WITH THE HULKSTER AFTER *BASH*

This was tough. No doubt, one of the hardest moments of my entire wrestling career. The last time I had seen Hulk was at *Bash at the Beach*, and we all know the history behind that. Knowing Hulk was all about business, I never really knew how much of his defamation lawsuit against me was personal, or, by piggybacking it in, was it just a way to strengthen his more lucrative lawsuit against WCW. Later, I would find out that it was indeed the latter, but going into this first meeting . . . I had no idea.

The meeting was to take place at some fancy hotel close to Hulk's home in Florida. I can remember, prior to it, Eric had me meet him in a local bar for the preamble. There is a reason that I remember this. That hour or so that I spent with Eric that day was the most memorable hour we ever spent together in our now 25-year history. For whatever reason, at that meetup, Eric came across as vulnerable to me—the first time he had ever presented himself in such a light. He explained to me the circumstances under which he had been fired from WCW, going into a meeting thinking he was "King Shit," while those who invited him had a much different picture. Eric made it clear that the experience humbled him—he just never saw it coming.

I don't know why Eric decided to open up to me that day, but for the first time, and the last time, I saw a real person.

From there, we went to the hotel to meet Hulk. When we arrived at his room, I was quite nervous, having no idea of the person I was going to encounter on the other side of that door. Was I going to get one of those wrestling promos that he had mastered over all those years, or was I going to get the *real* Terry Bollea? At that point . . . your guess was as good as mine.

I remember walking in and taking a seat. This was very reminiscent of the two-on-one encounter I had faced that day in Hulk's trailer at *Bash*. I remember—as much as I hated it—on this occasion, I knew I had to play the game. I couldn't just come out with what I really wanted to say, what had been building inside over the past nine years. I had to sit back and listen in order to understand their "game" because, in hindsight, that's all this was. The three of us were waiting on a chess board, trying to figure out the other's next move in an attempt to counter it before it was even made.

At this point, I really don't remember the specifics, and I'm not going to make something up in an effort to tell a good story. That's a "Bruce Prichard Move." I remember starting the conversation at *Bash*, talking about my POV of that day, then sitting back and listening to Hulk's version. Ironically, there was no argument over the facts—all three of us knew what the facts were. The day played out exactly as we discussed, with the only off-ramp being what I said in a fictitious wrestling promo. And how do we all know it was a fictitious wrestling promo? Simple—I never referred to Hulk as Terry Bollea, I referred to him as his character.

After addressing the elephant in the room, we went on to talk about TNA. Listening to Eric and Hulk, there was no question that their intentions were good—one hundred percent. They both came across not only as wanting to make a difference but as having no doubt in their minds that they would. At that point, I tried to smarten them up about how Dixie Carter conducted business. I wanted them to understand that no matter how pure and good their intentions were, Dixie's business prowess was certain to be an obstacle.

I first attempted to enlighten them about TNA finances. Everything we did in TNA was on a very tight budget. I vividly remember cutting Tara's (Lisa Marie Varon) tarantula, because we couldn't afford to pay its handler a couple hundred bucks a month. Eric had to know that this wasn't WCW, and the money just wasn't going to be there to accomplish some of the goals he may have had in mind.

Next, I informed them about perhaps Dixie's biggest flaw—the lack of confidence in herself to make impactful company decisions. From the time of her taking over the company, founder Jeff Jarrett succeeded in giving Dixie an inferiority complex when it came to her knowledge of wrestling and the wrestling business. If I'm going to be blatantly honest here, Jeff at times just made her feel flat stupid. This shook her confidence early on, thus making her afraid of making company decisions that she *needed* to make. Instead, Dixie would always look for somebody to make those decisions for her. The list in TNA's history of her right-hand men is never ending, from Jeff to JR, Eric Bischoff, Hulk Hogan, Bruce Prichard, John Gaburick, it was always somebody else making the important decisions about her company—not her. In my assessment of the situation, Dixie's lack of leadership and her failure to take responsibility was what would ultimately do her, and her company, in.

Before I go any further, I must say this: On a personal level, I don't have an unkind word to say about Dixie—not one. Having worked with her for some 10 years, I understand that Dixie was a victim of the wrestling business and the circus performers who came with it. She had no idea what she was getting herself into when she talked her wealthy father into investing in a company that lost its primary investor literally hours after its second show aired. Her intentions were good; she was just in way over her head.

The wrestling business wasn't for Dixie simply because she was a good woman with a good heart. The wrestlers saw that in her, and the majority of them took advantage of it. Unlike AEW's Tony Khan, Dixie wasn't a wrestling mark, and I wouldn't even consider her a money mark either. Her need to succeed was much more complicated than that.

You see, Dixie's dad, Bob Carter, founder of Panda Energy, ran an extremely successful company out of Texas. His son, Todd, was his right-hand man. Personally, I always felt that Dixie may have felt a sense of competition with her brother—perhaps trying to prove to her dad that she, not Todd, should have been the Chosen One. Ultimately, I think that was the driving force behind her running TNA. To prove to her father that she was just as worthy of his attention.

Ironically, I feel that Jeff Jarrett experienced the same sentiments with his father, Jerry, while Tony Khan experienced the same with his father, Shad . . . and throw Shane McMahon in there while you're at it. Man, that's a lot of pressure that each of those individuals put on themselves, constantly trying to prove their self-worth to the one who brought them into this world. I thank God that I never had that situation with my own father. My dad, to this day, accepts me for who I am . . . not what I did or didn't accomplish.

But, all-in-all, the meeting with Eric and Hulk went much smoother than I envisioned. But now the burning question: CAN WE ALL GET ALONG?

STREAM OF CONSCIOUSNESS

Back to that death thing.

I swear, man, I didn't mean to come back here . . . at least not this soon anyway . . . but under the guise of my stream of consciousness, the Grim Reaper has once again taken over my thoughts. It's been just a couple of days since wrestling legend Kevin Sullivan passed away.

Going back to *Rope Opera*, I spoke openly then about how both Kevin Sullivan and J.J. Dillon were undermining me when I worked at WCW. I also spoke about the hellacious promo I cut on J.J. as I stood within the wooden doorframe of his Smyrna office. Yeah, that's what the wrestling business will do to you.

Fortunately, when I was able to finally get away from it, I saw J.J. at a wrestling convention and had the opportunity to apologize. He graciously accepted the olive branch, and we have been good since.

Years later, following the demise of WCW, I actually had Kevin on my podcast. I held no animosity towards him whatsoever. It's wrestling, man, I understand that. Sometimes it affects people in ways that they aren't proud of. It just tends to get its hooks in you, working your mind, mouth, soul, and emotions. It's called being in the fire. The good thing: once that fire is extinguished, you can start acting like a civilized human being again.

Kevin Sullivan was a trailblazer—truly decades ahead of his time. The Taskmaster was doing edgy when edgy wasn't even a thing. He was fearless, never afraid of the ramifications of what his booking might bring. He was cutting edge, controversial, and pretty damn cool. His "booker man" angle with the late Brian Pillman was something like I had never seen before. He was both the NWO and the Attitude Era years before either existed. He was a one of a kind. He was special.

Just days after his death, I received a call from Dave Hodgson, a producer from Vice's *Dark Side of the Ring*. I have formed a good relationship with Dave over the years, as he has tapped into me for numerous *Dark Side* projects. I think I have made it on Dave's "Good List" because after working with hundreds of wrestlers on these docs I suspect he realizes that Ol' Vinnie Ru is one of the truthful ones. Anyway, Dave was calling to ask me if I wanted to be a part of the Daffney (Shannon Spruill) documentary that Vice was going to be producing in its next season of *Dark Side*. Word had gotten to Dave that I had a close relationship with Daffney, working with her first at WCW and then inviting her to join TNA once I became a part of that company.

Yeah, man, it's cliché, but, Shannon Spruill was an Angel. She was a blaring, blinding, magnificent white light in a very dark, dreary, hopeless world. She was an actress, a comedian, an entertainer, and one of the best all-around performers I had ever worked with. Just the sight of her would put a smile on my face, despite whatever daily struggles and stress I was experiencing at the time. My visit to NYC to shoot vignettes with Daffney, David Flair, and Crowbar (Chris Ford) for the "Ric Flair family album" angle was far and away one of my most memorable and enjoyable experiences in that company.

Daffney just got it. She knew wrestling was based on entertainment, and night in, night out she gave a standing-ovation performance. But, for Daffney, as is the case for many wrestlers, things would turn dark.

Daffney suffered severe head trauma in a match that included Raven and Abyss, and she would never be the same again. I remember watching that match on a monitor in the back, not knowing what they had laid out prior. In real-time, I witnessed Daffney in the middle of an extremely dangerous spot, one that just wasn't necessary to the overall end result. I remember meeting her as she came through the curtain, yelling at her for putting herself in such a dangerous position. That promo came out of a place of love—I truly cared about her welfare and well-being. Unfortunately, at that time . . . little did I know that night would be the beginning of her end.

I can't tell you how many times I witnessed this in my years in wrestling—the performers going over their match in the back and laying out spots that were both dangerous and unnecessary. On many occasions, when I had the time, I would have wrestlers lay out their matches to me and after listening to the risky spots they had planned I would say without hesitation, "no . . . you're not doing that." Somebody had to be responsible; somebody had to protect them from themselves.

Wrestlers have a habit of thinking they are invincible when it comes to laying out matches. They have a tendency to raise the bar, and then raise the bar even higher, until there's just nowhere left to go. Now, imagine being the single female in that male equation. You're not going to say no. You can't say no. They'll think you're weak . . . because you're a female. And Daffney didn't say no that night, and it may have cost her her life.

These are the things that just stay with you, much like my very last phone call with Daffney. That conversation took place about three months prior to her death. During that call Daffney was distraught, even broken. She was just coming off a lawsuit pertaining to the concussions and head trauma that she suffered in the ring. I don't want to get into the details—I honestly don't know what I can and can't discuss—but she was at a point where she wanted to tell her story and she felt that my podcasting platform would have been the perfect place to do that.

Many times during that conversation, Daffney broke down. She was wounded . . . deeply. Never once during that call did I think she was suicidal; if I did, I would have done more. I remember specifically her telling me about a storyline that stayed with her all these years. One that hurt her . . . scared her deeply.

That storyline was mine.

I remember there was a match at TNA, where the objective was for the loser to be embarrassed by having to peel down to their undergarments. The idea was that Daffney, the babyface and favorite, would lose the match, which would have been a surprise to the audience. When I wrote this, the idea I had in mind was comedy—hundred-percent comedy. What would the character, Daffney, do in that situation? In my mind, I thought that Daffney wouldn't know what to do, but with the crowd cheering her on, she would do a burlesque-type striptease, theatrically removing layers of her clothing, till she was down to her . . . granny panties. It was simply meant as a joke.

After she finished talking about it, I reminded her that it had been my idea, and that the intent of the scene was to be nothing but pure comedy.

But that segment really bothered her, and it had stayed with her throughout the years.

Needless to say, now I was broken. If only she would have relayed to me her uneasiness at the time, we just wouldn't have done it—it wasn't important. But that's just another thing about wrestlers. Many times they are hesitant to say no, out of fear of losing their spot. That was always ridiculous to me. Yeah, maybe that's the way it was "back in the day," but not once when I had the pencil for all those years did anybody lose their position on the card because they expressed feeling uncomfortable about doing something I wrote—never.

That just wasn't me. You write the shit, and there are a million different ways you can craft it. Rarely is anything ever so important that there isn't any other way to do it. That's why I always worked *with* the talent. I never dictated anything to them—I just didn't work that way. Now, if I thought you were being oversensitive about something, I would tell you, but I never forced anybody to do anything if they had good reason not to.

That conversation with Daffney stayed with me a long time. It concluded with me committing to helping her develop her own podcast. I left asking her to write a brief outline about exactly what she wanted her show to be, and then we would circle back. Unfortunately, that follow-up meeting never transpired.

I think I was actually online when somebody smartened me up about Daffney doing a live stream while brandishing a gun. Needless to say, I immediately went into panic mode and feverishly called her. She didn't answer. I then went back online and told everyone that I could to send Daffney messages telling her how much they loved her and how important she was to them. And they did. I went to bed that night not knowing the outcome of this horrific story.

I remember waking up the next morning, after not much sleep, and going online to make sure there wasn't any tragic news. Nobody was saying anything. Not knowing was tying my stomach in knots. All I could tell myself was "no news is good news." Then I received a DM from Daffney's good friend and ECW legend Francine. Francine informed me that Daffney had taken her own life the night before.

As I'm typing this, it still doesn't register. How could somebody so loving and full of joy end her life . . . and in such a horrific, violent manner. Daffney knew that the trauma she suffered in the ring had done permanent damage to her brain. One of her last wishes was for her brain to be donated to science and studied in order for everybody to understand the lasting effect that concussions could have on professional wrestlers. Daffney pulled the trigger of a loaded gun aimed into her chest . . . so her brain could be saved.

I miss her, man. I miss her so much. God bless you, my angel above.

6 ERIC'S ROLE IN TNA

During my adult life, I came to a point where I grew a great disdain for the word *liar*. To be more specific, the hatred of that word really materialized during my wrestling years.

I guess the reasoning behind this would be two-fold. For starters, in the wrestling business, I worked with dozens of them. It just always seemed like no one told the truth in the wrestling business . . . unless you were from New York, of course. Secondly, I can't tell you how many times my adversaries have labeled me that throughout my entire wrestling career. Vince Russo just lies about everything. Now, keep in mind, a hundred-percent of these accusations are backed with neither facts nor examples. Yeah, my enemies just like to refer to me as a liar.

Meanwhile, in my 34 years in the wrestling business, nobody has ever caught Vince Russo in a lie. That headline just doesn't exist. Why? Because I don't lie. There is just no reason to—especially when it pertains to pro wrestling. Nothing could be that important in pro wrestling to lie about . . . not to me, anyway.

So being on the opposite side of that accusation for so many years, I've grown to despise that word. So much so that I hate labeling anybody a liar, even when I'm 99 percent sure they are one. There's always that one percent chance they're not, and honestly . . . you just never know.

Except in pro wrestling.

In pro wrestling everybody is lying to you—every day, even on weekends. It's just the way of life in "the bubble." It's habitual; they just can't help themselves. So, when it came to Eric Bischoff's "official" role in TNA . . . somebody lied.

I've got to digress for a moment. I recently read a transcript from Eric's podcast, *83 Weeks*, co-hosted by Conrad Thompson, where he explained that he never wanted to go to TNA. The only reason he did was because Hulk asked him to handle all of his business affairs for him at the time. How that translated into Eric riding Hulk's coattails to get a job with the company is the story of a power play the two of them used dozens of times over the years.

Dixie wasn't interested in hiring Eric for TNA; she wanted Hogan, feeling that his superstar status would help put her company on the map. But, you know the play, man: "Oh, I can't come in without Eric . . . BROTHER." Bubba the Love Sponge, whom you'll read more about later, told me recently that Hulk was actually trying to talk Dixie into firing me and letting Eric take over the weekly TV writing. Yeah, that would have been good—Aces and Eights for 10 years.

But if I'm being fair, I don't blame Hulk for trying to get his sidekick a job. I mean, if you can finagle a six-figure salary for your friend to come along for the ride . . . all the power to you. No, I blame Dixie for hiring him. But make no mistake about it—she was *played* by two of the best in the game.

In that same interview, Eric also spoke about "being at the mountaintop," referring to the WWE, and asked aloud why would he want to "go somewhere that was clearly the minor leagues?"

THUS—YOUR PROBLEM.

If Eric really didn't want to go to TNA in the first place, thinking that he was "above it," then went anyway, what did anyone expect the end result was going to be? A lawsuit, perhaps? Well, that's exactly how the relationship ended with Eric, Dixie, and TNA: Easy E suing his former boss and her company.

But wait, hit those brakes, we're getting way ahead of ourselves here.

So, what exactly was Eric's role to be, in a creative sense, when it came to his position at TNA? Well, the way Dixie explained it to me was quite simple: "Eric would only be involved in 'HULK'S CREATIVE.' When it came to the rest of the show—he would have nothing to do with it."

Yeah, man, "situations" always begin with this bullshit. No different than the time WCW head honcho Brad Siegel told me that he wanted Eric Bischoff and me to "work together" when he told Eric something completely different—according to Eric, anyway.

But, at that point in time, I trusted Dixie. She was one of the few in the business that hadn't lied to me . . . yet. On top of that, I didn't want to be a problem for her. When I told her that it was her company and she could hire anyone she wanted to, I meant it. Hey, man, I'm the kind of guy who will try to make things work—but if they don't, I'll just leave. It was that simple for me.

So . . . that's how it started. Ed Ferrara, "Young" Matt Conway (a writer that I groomed at TNA), and I would sit in a meeting room with Eric and discuss Hulk's creative. And at the beginning it all went according to plan.

For almost two weeks . . . anyway.

So, here's the play, remember I was already *quite* familiar with Eric's shtick due to being at the receiving end at WCW over a decade prior. Here's how it works inside Eric's mind:

> I'll sit in the Creative meetings and act like the model "team" player. I'll only interject myself when it comes to "Hulk's creative." Then, once the meeting breaks, um . . . I don't know, maybe I'll grab a cream soda first, but soon thereafter I will meet with Dixie—one-on-one—and tell her that Vince doesn't know *WHAT THE F*** HE'S DOING*. And she'll buy it. She'll buy it because she's naive and because I, Eric, am one of the best workers in the business . . . have been for years.

Can you imagine burying the guy whose creative almost single-handedly put you out of a job at WCW? The guy who lapped circles around you while you were serving up the same stale nWo lunch meat for what seemed like eons? What does that say about YOU? I swear, I didn't know what was worse, Eric playing that lame, tired hand or Dixie picking it up and buying it—like she apparently did.

So, that's how it began. Eric would sit in on the creative meetings, getting himself more and more involved from a creative standpoint. And, let it be known . . . it wasn't just me. None of us liked Eric, none of us trusted him. And if you think I had an issue with him, Ed Ferrara practically threw up in his own mouth every time Eric would begin to even look like he was going to speak.

I'll never forget one of my all-time favorite encounters between Ed and Eric. This was at a time, about three to four weeks in, where Hulk was starting to get jobs for all his buddies. That's the game, man. How many times have you heard this story, and from how many different people? You know how this works. So, on this particular day, Eric brings up . . . the Nasty Boys. Now please, let me make one thing clear: I was a total mark for the Nasty Boys. During their heyday in both WWF and WCW, they had great runs, made a lot of cash. On top of that, Brian Knobbs is truly one of the nicest guys you will ever meet. Guy's a freaking sweetheart. But now, we're talking perhaps a decade past their prime. Man, you could tell by the look on Eric's face—this was so hard for even him to pitch. He knew it was bullshit, but part of his purpose of being there was to get Hulk's boys spots on the roster.

"What do you guys think about the Nasty Boys?" Eric asked.

Come on—what do you think we think? We think the same thing *you* think, I thought to myself. Unfortunately, Fast Eddie wasn't keeping his thoughts to himself.

Ed: "Are they still even a draw, Eric?"

Man, I can't wait to hear the response to this one—again, talking to myself.

Red in the face, and biting his lip, Eric asked, "What's a draw, Ed?"

It was in that instant I could see the Jersey in Ed come out. It was as if he'd been waiting for this moment for weeks. As my good friend Stevie Ray would say, "It's gonna be on like a steamin' pot of neck bones!"

Ed: "You know, Eric, a DRAW. Does anybody still care about the Nasty Boys?"

This was about as blatant as it gets. Ed was calling Eric out, and brother I've got to tell you firsthand, when you make the decision to call Easy E out, you are going to pay the price for the next two and a half decades.

This was foreshadowing the future of my relationship with Eric Bischoff—the destruction that continues to this day. We know you don't want the Nasty Boys here—just as much as we don't—but Hogan's your gravy train, and you're always going to attach your wagons to Hulk, even though you know this is not the best thing for business. I'm all for the loyalty thing, but at the end of the day, it's business and you should be doing what's best for business and what's best for the company you work for over what's best for a friend. You know how many people are mad at me to this day because I never gave them a job? Still, I guess I tip my hat to him for that. He knew his role, accepted it, and he was going to fulfill it to the best of his abilities.

This one exchange was the first of many future lines to be drawn in the sand. These few sentences spoke volumes about how we all felt having to work with each other. And, again, this falls on Dixie, not Eric. Dixie didn't want Eric, but Hulk full-court pressed and she hired him, even knowing there was ugly history between him and me—what on God's green earth did she think was going to happen?

But, here—here is where I give props to Eric Bischoff. He was doing exactly what Hulk wanted him to do, even though he himself knew it was a joke. That's true loyalty.

Kudos.

STREAM OF CONSCIOUSNESS

I need to break away from this story for a minute. In that last chapter I went in hard on Eric, and going into this book I promised that I wasn't going to do that. But I can't take it back. I can't take any of it back. If I did, then I wouldn't be being truthful, and I would be doing those who bought this book a great disservice.

And that's what writing has always done to me. The truth always comes out, no matter how good my intentions are. It's all inside. It's all bottled up inside. The death of my mother, the politics, the abuse from the marks, the lies, the deceit, the backstabbing, the disservice to my own family, the unappreciation, my mortality, the list is endless.

It's truly a double-edged sword. Writing is painful at times . . . no . . . it's painful much of the time. But at the same time . . . it's freeing. You've got to get that shit out—you've got to get it all out. If you don't take the time to cleanse your soul, it will just rot within you until you are dead inside. That's why I don't hold any anger, or vigor, it's just unhealthy, man. I needed this. I needed this badly.

7 WORKING WITH HULK

I'm going to give a stat here that might be a hard pill for many of you to swallow. With all the bullshit you've read about me and Hulk Hogan over the years, do you know that since I first worked with Hulk in 1999, he and I never once had one cross word between us? Not one. There was never an argument, difference of opinion, expression of opposing viewpoint. Every time there was ever a one-on-one exchange between Hulk and me, it was always very cordial, if not friendly.

So, Vince, you might ask, then what was the issue? Well, the issue was quite simple . . . the issue was Eric. I have stated on the record many times that I sincerely believe if it weren't for Hulk's friendship with Eric, he and I would have had a respectful working relationship. Once Eric Bischoff came into my life, he damaged a lot of my relationships. Everywhere I went, Eric would bury me to everybody behind my back.

Here's the list of those who counted the most:

WCW:

- Hulk Hogan
- TBS/TNT executive Brad Siegel

TNA:

- Hulk Hogan
- Dixie Carter
- Spike executive Scott Fishman
- Spike executive Kevin Kaye

Now how do I know this to be factual? Well, it's well documented that while I was working for WCW, Eric was petitioning Brad Siegel hard to get his job back, and at TNA, I had a great relationship with the liaison between Spike TV and TNA, Scott Fishman, before Eric arrived on the scene. Add to that, once Eric Bischoff became the executive producer of TNA (which I suggested and backed), Spike TV president Kevin Kaye ripped me publicly for no apparent reason. Hell, I never had even one conversation with that guy.

Eric was just hell-bent on slandering my name, smearing my reputation, and ultimately putting me out of work. Why? It was all a revenge game. I was the guy who broke the "83 weeks," I was the guy who took the luster off of him to his bosses at WCW, and I was the guy who would ultimately be responsible for him losing his position there. And, yeah, I was the guy who took his head of creative spot at that very same company.

Those reasons are on the surface. There were deeper roots for Eric's absolute hatred towards me that I will get into a bit later.

But Hulk and I? One-on-one, face-to-face, there was never an issue between us. This is where the misconception comes in. Based on a fictitious wrestling promo, there are many people who believe—to this very day—that I loathe the Hulkster with every ounce of venom in my body, but nothing could be further from the truth. Those who know me know when asked "who's at the front of your Mount Rushmore?" without any hesitation—and despite me closely working for years with "Stone Cold" Steve Austin and Dwayne "The Rock" Johnson—the answer is always Hulk Hogan.

I lived it, man; I lived through the "original" Hulk Hogan era. I didn't just hear about it, read about, watch old video on it . . . I experienced it. And, if you were a wrestling fan in the '80s—live and in person—you fully understand the impact that Hulk had not only on wrestling but on pop culture and the entire world. Everybody knew who the Hulkster was—everybody. His popularity at that time matched that of any big box office actor, superstar athlete, lead singer/rockstar of any band you could name—he was just THAT BIG. Maybe even bigger than our own president at the time!

That's why, no matter what went down backstage, I always treated him with the utmost respect. I never forgot who he was, or what he accomplished, and I haven't even to this very second.

But, what could have been never was. I swore to myself that I wouldn't make this about Eric, but there's no getting around it—it was all about Eric and his absolute disdain, hatred, animosity, envy, jealousy—whatever you want to label it—towards me. If it were indeed personal and I had disrespected him in any way, I would totally understand, but never did I ever do or say anything that would have been cited as a personal attack on him. Never once did I talk behind his back. As a matter of fact, the most heat I ever got with him was when I confronted him head-on, not once, but twice. Yet another topic that I will get into later in this book.

8 VINCE RUSSO: PATHOLOGICAL LIAR

"Vince Russo is a pathological liar."
—Eric Bischoff

I cannot tell you how many times Eric Bischoff has used the phrase pathological liar over the years when describing me.

Before we go any further, let's get the true, dictionary definition of what exactly a pathological liar is. According to the definition on Wikipedia around the time of writing,

> pathological lying, also known as *pseudologia fantastica* (Latin for "fantastic pseudology"), is a chronic behavior characterized by the habitual or compulsive tendency to lie. It involves a pervasive pattern of intentionally making false statements with the aim to deceive others, sometimes for no clear or apparent reason, and even if the truth is beneficial to the liar. People who engage in pathological lying often claim to be unaware of the motivations for their lies.

To sum this up, this would mean that I lie all the time. Now, I would have to think from a logical perspective, that whether you're a pathological liar, or just your average, run-of-the-mill liar, what is the one thing you fear the most? Simple: getting caught. Nobody wants to get caught in a lie because if you do, you're exposed, and the gig is up.

OK, so let's stick with logic. I'm a guy huge on logic. Logic makes sense . . . it always makes sense. So, if Vince Russo is a pathological liar, as Eric Bischoff suggests, then why would Vince Russo openly and publicly invite and accept a one-on-one conversation, with Eric Bischoff, where Easy E could easily expose him? Why would Vince ever do that? Illogical, don't you think? On top of that, why wouldn't Eric accept? What would be a bigger victory for him than exposing Vince Russo as a pathological liar? Again, rather illogical that he wouldn't jump at the offer.

None of it really makes any sense, does it?

And, according to Eric's description of me, then likely everything you've read in the first 34 pages of this book is an absolute lie—every bit of it. None of it happened, I'm just sitting here making all this shit up—for what, I have no idea—but I'm a pathological liar, so I must be.

You know, everything that I say, or write, I'm always prepared to back up with facts. Well, here are the facts:

A few years back, Conrad Thompson, whom I both respect and admire, was putting together "Ric Flair's Last Hoorah Weekend." As he was booking the event, Conrad, who is also the co-host of Eric's *83 Weeks* podcast, contacted me with a proposition. Conrad asked me if I would be open to a LIVE DEBATE with Eric Bischoff. Conrad stated that the two of us could "work" it out between us, something he felt it was not only what the fans would want to see, but he also stated that he felt it would be a huge moneymaker.

Without hesitation, I told Conrad I was one hundred percent on board. I was in. Now again—logic—does that sound like the response that a pathological liar would give when asked if he would be open to coming face-to-face, live, with his accuser? Or would that pathological liar instead be running, full speed, away from Nashville, Tennessee, where the event was going to taking place?

Once I gave Conrad my answer, he told me that he was going to have Eric call me. Again, if I'm being totally honest here . . . I know, I know,

I'm a pathological liar, but hypothetically, if I were being totally honest here, I knew there was no way in hell Eric was ever going to call. Why? Because I had made that same offer many times before, and every time he has either side-stepped it or ignored it. Many times, his excuse would be, "Why would I debate Vince? Every word out of his mouth would be a lie."

So I waited. No call. Conrad even called me back and asked if Eric had called—I said no. Wait a little longer. Nothing. "Ric Flair's Last Hoorah" in Nashville came and went, without a Vince Russo–Eric Bischoff debate.

Now, call me crazy, and I don't know about you, but, if I'm publicly calling somebody a pathological liar for almost 25 years, and I have the facts to back my claims, wouldn't I give my left NUT to confront said pathological liar? Wouldn't I want to expose him to the entire world? Embarrass him? Humiliate him? Any normal human being would jump at that opportunity. I've done that time and time again, for example when Meltzer or Prichard have blatantly lied about me. I first presented the facts to prove they were lying, then even invited Meltzer to a conversation (I couldn't invite Bruce because he was working for the WWE, and I knew it would be an impossibility), which, of course, he didn't want any part of.

So why, *why* after all these years does Eric Bischoff REFUSE to have a conversation with me?

I don't know . . . Could it be, maybe—just maybe—I'm not the one who's the pathological liar?

9 WHY I DON'T LIE

Before I get into some deep thought here, I first want to say that if you're one of my adversaries who want to believe that I am indeed a liar, then believe away. I truly understand that if you want to look at anybody in a particular light, good, or bad, that's the way you're going to view them regardless of what logic or facts are put forward. And that's your prerogative. But I can't tell you the number of people I have met over the years who've said to me, "Man, Vince, based on what I *heard* (or *read*), I believed you were a total schmuck—but you're really a nice guy."

Yeah, no shit.

I am truthful to my own detriment. In fact, it was telling the truth that got me heat in the wrestling business on more occasions than one. Whether I told somebody that I didn't see them as a top guy, or I didn't think their match was good, or they need to change . . . whatever—fill in the blank—if they ever want to get over with Vince McMahon, people in general just either don't want to hear the truth or flat out can't handle it. I was always the opposite.

Coming from a loud, Italian American family, you were always serving up the truth. And there was never any dancing around it; it was always up-close, personal and IN YOUR GRILL! That's just the way it was. That's just the way I was raised. I often say it's a New Yawk thing, because it is. New Yorkers are just no-nonsense, don't give me the bullshit, type of people.

That's why the thought of lying about anything associated with pro wrestling is a joke to me. It's just not important enough to lie about. Hell, I've publicly claimed some of the biggest failures in the history of the business as my ideas. Failures like the Kennel from Hell match, the Stairway to Heaven abomination, even poor, innocent and sweet Beaver Cleavage, I have zero problem saying those gargantuan misses came from my genius brain. Whereas if I truly were a liar, there were/are at least half a dozen others I could point to and deflect blame.

If you have to lie, I can only think of three reasons why.

1. Cheating on your wife. Let me be clear I have been married to the same woman for over 40 years, and never once have I ever cheated on Amy—never even came close. Even having been around cheating for years, courtesy of "the boys." Cheating on your wife while she was home raising your kids while you were off playing wrestling is the greatest disrespect you could ever show anyone.
2. Murder. No, never murdered anyone either. But I guess if you did, you might lie about it.
3. To not hurt someone else's feelings. Now, this I'm certain I've been guilty of. Telling anyone the truth about themselves is extremely difficult. However, if you are doing it in an effort to make them a better person for it—it's worth doing.

10 ERIC/HULK'S FIRST TNA SHOW

There was much hoopla surrounding Hulk Hogan's first TNA show. I remember he didn't appear on the show immediately after he signed; his first appearance was built up for a few weeks. During that stage, Eric really was concerning himself just with Hulk's creative, but as I stated in the last chapter, his boundaries didn't stay controlled for long.

During that period, Hulk appeared on *Larry King Live* wearing a TNA T-shirt, but I remember he was selling *himself* WAY more than he was his new company. Nevertheless, I knew Dixie was borderline orgasmic over this. It's really hard to describe her actions during the Hulk honeymoon period. Dixie was a hundred-percent convinced that the signing of Hulk was going to immediately put her in the game with Vince McMahon and the WWE.

I may have covered this in *Rope Opera*, but one of my favorite Dixie stories concerning the Hulkster is when, prior to the week of his TNA debut, Dixie had every one of her staff members DRESS UP LIKE HULK HOGAN at the weekly meeting. I swear to you, if I had been at the meeting, I would have lost my job. Understand, Dixie wasn't *asking*, she was *demanding*! There was no way in hell I would have ever met those demands if I was part of that meeting.

A week before Hulk's debut, there was a huge meeting at Spike TV headquarters, where Dixie and Eric laid out the Hulk Hogan Marketing Plan in full. No, of course Hulk wasn't there, but in his absence, Eric was propping him up on a pedestal, and the Spike execs were eating it like it was filet mignon and caviar with a fine, aged wine. Well, it was aged, but perhaps no longer fine. I swear, man, they were so excited over this *monumental* get that you would have literally thought that *Jesus himself* was going to appear on the show.

I remember sitting and thinking about the words Vince McMahon spoke to me seven years earlier, when I almost went back to the WWE and was concerned how he was going to handle my reunion with the Hulkster. Vince's words:

"I don't give a shit about Hulk Hogan, he hasn't drawn me a dime."

That was SEVEN YEARS EARLIER.

But I have to give credit where credit is due: Eric Bischoff played the role of P.T. Barnum better than Mr. Barnum played it himself. The Hulk hype-train was plowing through that office, and these incompetent bozos couldn't hop on fast enough.

As we got closer to showtime, more and more of Hogan's friends were being signed by Dixie. I remember Jeff Hardy, Scott Hall, Ric Flair, the Nasty Boys, of course . . . I don't remember who was signed when, but they all eventually made their way onto the show. All I could think about at the time was, Where the hell is she getting this money?

The very first night Hulk showed up on the show may have actually been the beginning of the end. Dixie was spending an exorbitant amount of money on this "Hulk project," money I knew that neither she nor her family had. She was banking *everything* into the red and yellow, and I don't know, maybe 20 years ago this would have been a good investment with Hulk in his prime, but *now*? This was a gamble to say the least.

The night of the show we all met at the same hotel where Hulk and I had our first meeting prior to his comeback tour. I remember this meeting vividly because this is where I first met Bubba the Love Sponge. Yes, Hulk had succeeded in getting his best friend, a radio DJ, a job as well. But, man, I'm not taking any swipes at Bubba. Despite the fact that he and Hulk buried me on air *daily* after *Bash at the Beach*, Bubba was great at what he did. The guy oozed charisma . . . as an entertainer, not a booker.

That's right—as six of us (me, Eric, Hulk, Bubba, Matt, and Ed) sat on two twin beds , Bubba the Love Sponge started booking the show! If you could have seen the eyeroll that Ed Ferrara threw my way, you'd still be cracking up 15 years later too. But, regardless, this dude was both entertaining and a CHARACTER, and you know how I feel about characters.

But Eric hated Bubba. Hated him. Even though, if I'm being honest here (which, again, I'm probably not being because of that "pathological" thing), Bubba was kind of a hard guy to hate. He had a charm about him, and he was !@#$%^& hysterical. Why do you think months later I personally would save him from the deadly clutches of Awesome Kong? (Another story I'll get into a little later.)

That night, there is no question, the show felt different. However, in my opinion it felt different because of the money that was added to bring in Hulk's family and friends. Of course we had more "star power," but at what expense? Again, Dixie Carter was no Tony Khan; there were no billions of dollars here. The fact is that she had to explain every expense to her parents, who would have to green light them first. Again . . . was that very first day the beginning of the end for Dixie Carter and TNA? Dixie had to be sweating over the money, she had to be. Damn, we had "Taco Tuesdays" going in catering just to save a buck! So, this would *have to* pay off for her.

My favorite memory of that night was that we had a match inside some kind of special dome-like structure we had built for the show. Man, this was a big night, so we were looking for a spectacle—but, again, I had no idea what this thing cost, I just know it wasn't cheap.

If you go back and watch that episode, I believe that Jeff Hardy made his first TNA appearance during this match, but the plan was to get Homicide (Nelson Erazo) over. I loved Homicide; a fellow New Yorker, of Puerto Rican descent, who absolutely oozed both character and charisma. He was also a great worker in the ring—perhaps a bit reckless here and there, but exciting out the wazoo! So earlier in the day, I approached Homicide on at least two, maybe three occasions and asked, maybe even *strongly suggested*, that he go out to the arena and become familiar with the cage—again, this wasn't your typical steel cage. Homicide assured me not once, not twice, but THREE TIMES, "Vince . . . no need . . . I got this."

Well, of course on LIVE TV, Homicide didn't have nothin'—he couldn't get out of the cage. I swear to you, he was hanging there like a drunken bat, not knowing where to go or how to get there. Now, whereas in itself that scene does come across as freakin' hysterical . . . at the time, it wasn't.

You have to remember that there were new sheriffs in town, and a screw-up on TV like this—Eric and Hulk could put a bullet through your entire career. Yeah, this was no longer the days of the fair-haired boy from Tennessee—Double J wasn't calling the shots anymore. It was Eric and Hulk. Not only did they have Dixie's ear, they had her head, her body, her shoes, and maybe even her car keys! Homicide could literally be done in seconds—I knew and understood this fully—which is why I'd wanted him to rehearse the spot.

But, through it all, the one thing that stood out to me that night was a five-second conversation that I had . . . one that I have never forgotten.

11 BERNIE

One of the things I enjoyed throughout my entire wrestling career was finding new talent. No, not in-ring talent, but rather the gifted people I worked with that nobody would ever know. In my first book, *Forgiven*, I dedicated an entire chapter to the great Richard Curtis, whom I worked with at the WWF. Richie was a magician by trade, and he was responsible for all the special effects the audience experienced while watching the product.

There was also such a person at TNA that I want to pay homage to, who also plays an important part in the timing of this story. Her name was Bernie . . . just Bernie. Bernie was an employee of Universal Studios, who was responsible for basically "keeping an eye on us" while we taped our shows at the Universal theme park in Orlando, Florida. Bernie was probably in her late 30s, early 40s, black-gray hair, very short in stature, who smoked like a freakin' chimney. The woman always had a tobacco stick hanging out of her mouth as if it were permanently attached to her lips.

At every TV taping, Bernie and I would play a game of cat and mouse. Every time she would turn her back on me, I would hunt out a cool location at Universal—one that we weren't cleared to use—then rush the talent on set and attempt to shoot something before Bernie showed back up. Then when she did, I'd play totally dumb, and she would give me a rap across my knuckles. Man, I loved working with Bernie—main reason being she had such a great work ethic and smile to go along with it.

So this was the first night of what was turning into the Hulk Hogan Show. Bernie was not a wrestling fan, so she had no idea who all these new people were. I remember being about halfway through the day when Scott Hall was just being Scott Hall: loud, obnoxious, and just busting somebody's balls. Man, I've talked about this before . . . I always respected Scott Hall, but at times he just wasn't fun to work with. You never knew what kind of mood he was in on any given day, and what kind of attitude would come out of it. Scott never made my job easy.

I remember after I was done with wrestling, I worked a convention that Scott Hall was a part of. That day, I approached Scott, and out of the blue asked him, "Scott, why do I feel like you just never liked me?" Scott said, "Because I never liked the fact that you get so much credit in the wrestling business and Eric gets none." I simply answered back, "And how is that my fault?" Scott had no answer.

But, getting back to that day, as I stated a few sentences ago, Bernie had no idea who theses new people were, nor did she care, and, perhaps more importantly, she certainly wasn't impressed. As Bernie and I walked a few yards behind Scott, Bernie turned to me and said, "Vince . . . things feel different. I don't have a good feeling about this."

Man, was Bernie spot on. That early in the Bischoff/Hogan Experiment, I just knew that this venture wasn't going to have a happy ending. This mix of people . . . we were just not going to be able to work side by side in harmony.

12 WHY THIS WAS DOOMED FROM THE JUMP

When you go back in history and look at why the Bischoff/Hogan era failed, it's pretty simple to understand. Prior to that "dream team" coming in, you had a company that was pretty much run a certain way—the Jeff Jarrett–Dixie Carter way—from 2002 through 2009. Now, whereas I thoroughly document their rocky relationship in my second book, at least that relationship was *consistent*. Those employed got used to the system—as dysfunctional as it was at times. And, though they had flaws (just as I have mine), everybody generally liked Jeff and Dixie.

Well, not exactly everybody.

Man, the TNA Knockouts had their issues with Dixie. And much of that had to do with her taking priority in hair and makeup when they had to get ready for the day's work and she wasn't even on the show! All the girls would have to wait until the owner of the company got all prissed up before they could get their hair and paint on to go to work. But that was really a minor issue. Dixie was liked, and even though that may have been attributed in part to us just feeling sorry for her due to the position she put herself in, as a person . . . she was well admired.

Jeff, on the other hand . . . was loved. Especially by the younger guys, whom he had given a great opportunity with TNA, for many their first and for some even their last. Now, the vets may have had some issues with Jeff always booking himself on top, but again, that fair-haired boy from Hendersonville had charisma. He balanced being the boss and one of the boys probably as well as anyone could. Jeff was approachable, his door was always open, and the boys never hesitated to walk in. And that laugh . . . that laugh would just put a smile on your face every time you were around it.

Enter Genghis Khan.

Eric Bischoff was a dictator. Eric got off on power. He loved that people feared him. He was arrogant, self-centered, full of himself, and, yeah . . . the total opposite of Jeff. So within the matter of just a few weeks, you were going from one extreme to the other. Whereas the boys, and much of the office were looking to "party" with Jeff after the show, those same people wouldn't even want to be in the same hotel as Eric.

Now, I just want to be clear here. Not everybody felt this way about Eric . . . I think he may have had some fans . . . but if he did, they couldn't fill the first five seats of the front row of the Impact Zone. And I think he wanted it that way; I think he even liked it that way. But the responsibility has to lie on the shoulders of the woman running the show . . . Dixie. How could she not see and understand that the dynamic of her entire company was going to change overnight? The writing was carved into the wall.

Dixie made this change out of pure desperation. This all goes back to her not wanting to make any decisions. She honestly believed that Hulk—not Eric—was the magic bean that was going to catapult her beanstalk to the next stratosphere. She couldn't have been more wrong. And, slowly, but surely, you would start seeing the signs of this absolute disaster about to come to fruition.

13 ERIC AND HULK'S FIRST PIECE OF DOOMED BUSINESS

You guys have had new jobs throughout your lifetimes, right? Well, you know how when you first get hired there's that "lay low" period of a few weeks where you just kinda fall in line, learn the system, make sure you don't rub anyone the wrong way, stay small, and keep your mouth shut?

Yeah . . . not Hulk and Eric.

It felt like it was within the first month that they had convinced Dixie Carter and the brass at Spike TV that *Impact*, TNA's flagship show, must go—had to go, head-to-head with the WWE's juggernaut *Raw*. My first response, "Are you !@#$%^& kidding me?"

I'll tell you why that was my knee-jerk. Forget their talent being better, forget that *Raw* was well established and had owned that timeslot on Monday night for decades, forget the WWE production value compared to the look of our show, forget all that. I knew that this move would be a total failure based on finances alone. We couldn't compete with the WWE and *Raw* simply from a monetary point of view. Everything they did was just going to be far superior overall just looking at the money they had to spend.

The Carters didn't have McMahon money, and if they did—then they weren't going to spend it. If you are going into a fight, then you must be prepared to compete at *every level* . . . there was just no way that TNA could.

Again, in an effort to show I'm being fair, I'll say here that really thought that both Hulk and Eric thought we had a chance. I never once felt this was a malicious effort on their part to try and break the bank.

Matt, Ed, and I were working on the show in our "box" on the top floor of the Holiday Inn Express when Dixie called to let me know. She was giddy. No . . . freakin' GIDDY. She was so excited about the idea of not only competing against Vince McMahon head-to-head but actually *beating* him, that there wasn't anything negative about the situation that I could say. I just had to let it play out until the experiment would come crashing down.

I remember when the numbers came in that first night. I think we did in fact draw a higher number just playing off the exposure we got from *Raw* by being a wrestling show in the same time slot at the same night, but that was it. When Dixie brought those numbers to Hulk and Eric, I could see the look on everybody's face. This thing was over before it even started.

I guess you can say "we tried," and if we hadn't we would have never known. But who are we kidding. If you moved AEW to Monday nights opposite *Raw* right now—what do you think that would look like?

But, putting all that aside, it's time to move on.

14 SIGNS, SIGNS, EVERYWHERE THE SIGNS

Within a couple of weeks, I quickly noticed a pattern. It was the same playbook that I experienced working with Eric at WCW . . . this is how it starts. And you know the guy—you all know the guy. At one point in your careers, no matter what you do for a living, you've all worked with him. You know, the dude who attends the meeting, throws out all his lame-ass ideas, then leaves the meeting, and you never hear from him again until after what was discussed in that meeting is put into a finalized plan, document, or in this case scripted.

At that point, here's the play:

Eric's concern was and rightfully should have been what Hulk was doing. Only problem was—he never had any idea. He never even presented a suggestion, even though the only reason he was supposedly there was to do that one thing. So, having to move the process along, we came up with ideas for Hulk that we would pitch to Eric and then let him sit on. We'd then go and write the other hour and 45 minutes of the show.

Ed Ferrara was an employed writer in Hollywood, penning such shows as *Honey, I Shrunk the Kids* and *Weird Science*. He taught me so freaking much, I would never be the writer I am today without his influence. So, here's the arrogance of Eric Bischoff—Matt, Ed, and I would write the show in its entirety, then we would have to send the completed show to Eric—per Dixie—just like Ed and I sent the completed showed up to Vince back in the WWF days. Here's my biggest pet peeve: don't freaking mark up all our shit in red and tell us it sucks when you don't have one single suggestion to make it better.

I learned that early on with Vince. I would never tell him something wasn't good unless I had something freaking better. I was trained that way. To Eric—this was a display of power. What he would do is redline everything, and send it back to us with not one suggestion. Not one way how he thought we could make it better. Then, we'd all have to sit there with our thumb up our ass waiting until he was available for us to talk to him while we're working against the clock. That freaking prick! You know these GoTo Meetings? He made me and Ed have one with him on Christmas Eve! Ed was ready to quit because we were trying to meet with him days and days beforehand. He was too busy with whatever other personal deals he had going on. Like selling wrestling-themed slot machines to casinos. Yeah—he did that.

This is what we were dealing with all the time. There's a show every week. This isn't like we're working on a movie. We got a show in two days—pick up the phone, and freaking call us! And Hogan's nowhere around during this time.

It could've well been possible that Hulk, himself, didn't even want to be involved in such power-play political bullshit. But that's Eric Bischoff to a T. I'll sit in on a meeting with you, share my wisdom and knowledge, but when it comes to doing the actual grunt work . . . I'll be relaxing at my posh hotel down the street from yours. No, I'm not exaggerating—while Ed and I stayed at a Holiday Inn EXPRESS, Eric stayed a mile down the road at one of the most posh, luxurious, and expensive hotels in Nashville. Why? Because Eric was BETTER than the hired help, that's why.

So, while Eric was doing who knows what in his suite, Ed, myself, and Matt Conway would write the show in a tiny conference room on the top floor of the hotel, which sat across from a McDonald's.

That's the Eric Bischoff way.

Man, that just grates on you. No matter what Eric thought of himself—he wasn't better. I am a firm believer that God created us all equal. What makes us unique individuals consists of many things—our parents, friends, experiences, situations, decisions, etc., but no one is *better* than anyone else, and Eric certainly wasn't better than the three slobs doing all the work.

This was the same exact scenario that led me and him down this very familiar path in WCW. You're either in the trenches or you're not, and if you're not—then just get the !@#$%^& out of my way. Come on, man, nobody likes this type of individual—nobody. Who wants to hang out with somebody who thinks they're better than you? And, again, there's Dixie meeting all his demands, the expensive hotel, no doubt he was flying first class, and who knows what other perks he was getting.

If you're questioning if maybe I was a bit jealous of the first-class treatment Eric always seemed to get, the answer is—I wasn't. Not one bit. Fact is that I loathe prima donnas, or divas—anyone who thinks they're better than you are. And not only was I not interested in "perks," but I was rather concerned with trying to save Dixie money. I didn't care what hotel I stayed in, I never flew first class even in the wrestling business (outside of Dustin and Terri Runnels once bumping me up on a flight to *Late Night with Conan O'Brien*). Eric's expectations and demands are everything I hate about white collars—everything. If you don't want to do the work, you're not going to have my respect, and if I'm going to be transparent here . . . Eric never had my respect.

But that was just the beginning of what would get my goat. Here's what really pissed me off. So, on the day of TV, we would have a production meeting at about 10 or 11 in the morning. Eric and Hulk would be part of that meeting, and to their credit they would always show up on time. During these production meetings we would discuss every aspect of that night's show. Eric and Hulk were active in those meetings, and that's a big point for them.

Wait . . . I'm being sidetracked.

STREAM OF CONSCIOUSNESS

I will never forget when in one of those meetings, Hulk was getting excited about a Jeff Hardy match that was being laid out. Now, if you know Hulk, you know his eyes get real wide when he's excited about something. Well, as Hulk jumps into the conversation with his two cents, he says the following—which was almost the title of this book:

"Yeah, brother, and then he hits him with the WONTON BOMB!"

Bro . . . come on. Of course what Hulk meant was Swanton Bomb, but he totally botched it. And guess what—NOBODY LAUGHED! We all looked at each other but, out of respect for Hulk, nobody laughed.

I digress.

So, getting back to the meeting, I'd say the average production meeting would last about 90 minutes. As soon as it was over, we'd go to catering, choke down our food, and start the stacked workday at about noon, which was the talent's call time. Those hours were *vital* to the show. During this time, I would go over everybody's parts of the show, give them their in-rings, match notes, produce the vignettes, etc. This was a *solid* six hours of nonstop work . . . for me.

Eric and Hulk . . . they were nowhere to be found during this time.

Gone—nowhere in sight. Where'd they go? Your guess is as good as mine. This is the pattern that took place, week after week after week. Then, come about an hour before showtime, the "dream team" would waltz in ready to start their excruciating night of work—after it had already been done for them. But, if that weren't enough, with 60 minutes to go before showtime . . . they would start CHANGING SHIT.

Are you starting to get the picture here? Are you starting to understand why I would eventually be driven off the deep end? You're either a part of the team, or you're !@#$%^& not. And what did Dixie do . . . ? Not a damn thing.

Shit like this was starting to crack me. I knew that I was only going to be able to stomach it for so long. Man, my entire life I have just hated when people would think they were better than you, and that's how Hulk and Eric were making me feel . . . like they believed they were better than everybody else.

15 MAJOR CRACKS

This new structure started to become unenjoyable, no, intolerable, in a hurry. Going back seven years, I turned down a consulting role with the WWE because I wanted to work with my friend Jeff Jarrett in his new start-up. Man, had that plan become derailed, and now the train was exploding off the tracks and heading straight towards disaster.

I just couldn't stomach the prima donna attitude of both Eric and Hulk. Prior to their arrival, yeah, TNA may have been a dysfunctional family—but we were still a *family*. By that I mean, for the most part, we truly cared about each other. Now, don't misread this, not everybody loved me either. I know Chris Daniels hated me, but that disdain came from my putting entertainment before wrestling, and, let's face it, that's all just a matter of taste.

As this started to become the norm, my frustration and displeasure over the situation were starting to mount. I could feel it in the pit of my stomach. What used to be an enjoyable job—well, as enjoyable as a job in wrestling could be—was turning into my worst nightmare. Flipping pizzas at Sbarro at 16 was a primo job compared to this mess. I now hated going to work, and I hated working with Eric Bischoff. And as much as I tried to put on my happy face, I wasn't kidding anybody—it was clear I no longer wanted to be there.

I was one cross word, or wrong look from blowing up . . . and that would come next over one particular incident. Here is a perfect example—remember, I follow everything up with facts—on how Hulk and Eric's self-serving schedule would affect the entire talent roster and show.

On the Universal Studios lot we were housed within, there was a green room where the top guys usually dressed. This would be the place where you could find Ric Flair, Kurt Angle, Sting, Booker, Mick, Nash, or whatever top guys were a part of the company at the time. On this particular night there was a huge match between Sting and Kurt that was going to headline the show. We had built up the angle for weeks, and this was the night we were going to pay it off.

Throughout the entire week, Kurt, Sting, and I were all in contact with each other, throwing ideas around and discussing how the match might be laid out. I remember both of them telling me that they tried to contact Hulk during the week, but he never got back to either one of them.

So now, day of the show, Sting and Kurt are laying out their match all afternoon. When they were finished, they laid it out to me—like they really needed to lay it out to me—and it all sounded great. What else would it be? We are talking about two of the greatest players to ever set boots in a ring. Sting and Kurt were eager to run it by Hulk. But wait . . . where's Hulk?

Soon it's 3 p.m., 4 p.m., 5 p.m. . . . where's Hulk?

Finally, about an hour before the show starts, Eric and Hulk saunter on in. I immediately grab Hulk and take him to the green room so Steve and Kurt can tell him what they've come up with. The two had spent all week on this one match, and they both felt confident that they had nailed it.

After the two Legendary Icons had presented their match, Hogan, without even taking a pause said . . . "What about this?" From there, he laid out something that was totally different from what Kurt and Sting had come up with. I remember as Hulk was rambling on, both of them looked at me with that "WHAT THE !@#$%^&" look. You could see it in their eyes: Where was he when we were trying to call him all week? An hour before the match he wants to change everything?

Now, guys, when I get in a situation like this, where my blood begins to boil, there is only one thing I can do before I pop the cork, and that's get up and leave. And that's exactly what I did. As Hulk continued to speak . . . I got up and walked out.

At that point, I just couldn't take it anymore. To me it was all about the total disrespect that Hulk showed not only me, but more so both Kurt and Steve. They had been working through the process all week, and he walks in at the 12th hour and shits on everything? Later that night, Dixie attempted to reprimand me for the very first time. I clearly remember getting so upset with her that I literally told her, "I will go home before I'm ever disrespected like that again."

This was all on her, man. She was letting Eric and Hulk play by their rules, not hers, but she couldn't expect me to play by them as well. You see, there was no confusion here like there was with Brad Siegel back in WCW—Eric Bischoff was not my boss, because if Dixie had told me he was, I would have exited the company immediately. This situation was about to go from bad to worse.

16 I NEED TO CHILL FOR A MINUTE

This is where I need to take a break. I promised myself that I wouldn't go down this road. I promised myself that NO MATTER WHAT—there would be no promos on Eric. That wasn't my goal, and that wasn't my intention. I guess I sorta, kinda thought I was over it . . . but . . . I guess I'm not.

If I'm going to be a hundred-percent honest, it would be almost impossible to write this book while keeping my true thoughts and feelings in check, in a concerted effort to try and be *nice* to Eric. No—a big eff that.

When it comes down to it, I guess I dislike Eric Bischoff as much as he dislikes me—maybe even more. But, I swear, up until the writing of this book, I had done a good job of putting it behind me. I thought I didn't hold a grudge against him, I thought I was over it, but it is obvious to anyone reading this—I still hold the same sentiments. My absolute animosity and disdain towards Eric are still alive and well deep within my soul.

Eric is probably the lone reason I fought myself over writing this book. I didn't want to talk negatively about him, really, but this is my truth and my story.

Thankfully, if I am the Pathological Liar that Eric claims I am, then none of what I'm saying is the truth, and I really *love* the man.

It all comes down to that one trait I have despised my entire life—people who are full of themselves. I don't understand why that, more than anything, just rubs me the wrong way. Eric is full of himself. He loves himself. He revels in his every thought and his every word. He was full of himself on that first phone call, that meeting at Hops 25 years ago, and on his own podcast just last week.

And, as I'm really going through some therapy here, my feelings are not the same towards Hulk. Even the "immortal" Hulk Hogan never carried himself with the conceit, pompousness, and arrogance that Eric did... and still does.

Yeah, I was really pissed with him over that one incident I just spoke about, but knowing Hulk, he probably didn't even realize he did anything wrong. Hulk was *not* an egotistical ass, he was *never* an egotistical ass, Eric always was.

And I want to apologize to him for saying that. Because for all I know, Eric could still be playing a character after all these years. That's the thing with wrestling lifers who live in the bubble: they literally come to a point of not knowing who they really are. Hulk has even admitted that, and so has Ric Flair. Jim Cornette has no idea where the Jim "character" ends and the "real" Jim begins. In my case, my character went bye-bye the last time you saw me in a wrestling ring on TV. That part was over for me, and there's never been any confusion since. But for some of these guys . . . I just don't know.

I've got to take a deep breath before I start up again. In these first 16 chapters, I have only scratched the surface. So much more is yet to come.

17

BUBBA VS. KONG

Yeah, man, let me take a breather from the Bischoff Burial to share with you a much lighter moment . . . even though it was much more severe at the time.

As I told you earlier, prior to working with him, Bubba the Love Sponge and Hulk were "besties." Hulk was constantly on Bubba's show, a wildly popular radio show in the Tampa area, where many a day the content was headlined by the thrashing of Vince Russo. Now, whereas Bubba didn't know me, never met me, never spoke to me, he was merely doing what any good friend would do—hate on the enemy of his brother. It's totally understandable. However, at the time, Bubba never dreamed that not only would there come a time where he and I would be face-to-face but one where we would actually be working together.

Upon meeting Bubba for the first time, I honestly didn't know what to expect. Was he going to be brash and insulting "Radio Bubba," or was he going to be a decent human being? Much to my amazement, he was the latter. From the moment we met, Bubba was always respectful towards me and I was towards him; who knows, maybe it was the bond we had in both loathing Eric Bischoff. And, shockingly, despite all the prior radio hate that Bubba threw my way for years—I actually liked him and enjoyed talking to him. BUT—did I like him enough to SAVE HIS LIFE?

So, one day, I'm producing a pre-tape backstage at Universal. In the distance I could hear some quarreling, even scuffling. My first thought was that two of the boys were going at it, even though that rarely ever happened. So, sniffing a situation, I immediately hurried over to the scene. What I witnessed, I will never forget.

As I got closer to the disturbance, I could see Awesome Kong all over Bubba like a hungry bear devouring an unsupervised picnic basket!!! I mean, she was *mauling* him. Bubba was a human speed bag to her windmill of wild rights and lefts. To Bubba's credit, he did not attempt to fight back; he simply attempted to protect himself until Mama Bear tired herself out. Not knowing the right thing to do, I did the only thing I could—I put my arms around Kong and pulled her off the shocked, surprised, and battered Bubba. The cause of this outburst? Apparently, Kong felt she had been disrespected by Bubba through some comments he made on his morning show. Throughout my 20 years in the active wrestling business, that was only the second fight I ever had to break up. The first was Luna Vachon and Sunny, which, you can imagine . . . wasn't much of a fight at all.

To this day, Bubba and I stay in touch under much different circumstances. He and Hulk are no longer friends, ever since the infamous Hulk Hogan sex tape scandal, where Hulk was filmed by a hidden camera in Bubba's house while making whoopee to the shock jock's wife!!! Hulk would wind up suing Gawker, who bought and distributed the tape, and win millions in court, which forced them to ultimately close their doors. It was later proven that Bubba had nothing to do with selling the tape to Gawker—in fact, it was stolen from his house by an employee of his.

Ironically enough, over the years Bubba and I have become friends, when years later I would go to his defense over information he was given concerning the declining health of Hulk. Whereas nobody believed what he was reporting, I certainly did, knowing Bubba had just too much specific information, had no reason to lie, and would have been sued out the wazoo if he had.

But yeah, for the record—Bubba *still* owes me for saving his life!

18 ERIC BISCHOFF IS NOT CREATIVE

I just saw comedian Rob Schneider, of *SNL* fame, on an interview with Tucker Carlson. Schneider said: "You know you're *out* when a new regime comes in."

And there lies the problem in its purist form.

When Dixie made the decision to bring in Hulk Hogan and Eric Bischoff—with whatever promises and commitments she made to them—she should have also come to the realization that the Vince Russo era of TNA was over—even though that was clearly not her intention when she hired the "dynamic duo." Matter of fact, Bubba would confirm to me years later that he was present when a phone call took place between Hulk and Dixie prior to Hulk being hired, where Hulk was matter-of-factly trying to sell Dixie that Eric should take over TNA creative—which of course was my job at the time. To her credit, Dixie ixnayed that push.

When any new coaching regime is brought in by any NFL team, the entire old coaching staff goes bye-bye so the new coach can have a fresh start. Not only is that *business*, but I agree with it, one hundred percent.

I'm going to be totally transparent here—when Dixie Carter sent Jeff Jarrett home from TNA because she found out that Jeff and Karen Angle were involved in a personal relationship (even though, Jeff will tell you, the Angles were separated at the time), I believe that Dixie expected me to work hand-in-hand with Jim Cornette. Up until that time, Jeff had always been the buffer between me and Cornette, to assure that nothing ever got out of hand. And it never did, partly because Jim would never say or do anything to my face . . . but more importantly both of us had the utmost respect for Jeff.

When Dixie brought that up, I wanted to tell her that she was !@#$%^& nuts, but what I actually told her was that that would be completely unfair to me. Cornette hated my booking and hated my style from day one; no way he wouldn't have been a deterrent, attempting to undermine me while I was trying to do my job. In other words, James E. Cornette was never going to be on Team Russo.

Dixie abided, and she released Jim from the company. There was never an ultimatum put forth by me—I don't work that way. If Dixie had kept Jim around and the inevitable happened . . . I would have just left the company, just like I left when the Hogan/Prichard/Bischoff "dream team" became too unbearable to handle.

It was almost a decade earlier when Brad Siegel did the same thing at WCW. When Siegel brought Eric back on at WCW, he didn't release me from my contract; he "thought" that Eric and I would be able to work together. Siegel should have just relieved me of my duties at that point, paid my contract in full, let me go my merry way, and let Eric be his new captain. But he didn't. Why? Because, I believe, neither Brad, at the time, nor Dixie, was a hundred-percent on board with Eric and both wanted to keep me around as a "safety net"; not only was I more manageable to work with, but they knew that I understood the ins and outs of creating, writing, scripting, formatting, and producing a successful wrestling show for prime-time television.

Come on, man, you hear the stories from everybody and anybody that worked with Eric at WCW. There was no structure, no planning, everything was by the seat of their pants. They would literally be writing and rewriting the show less than an hour prior to going live. When I first arrived on the scene at WCW, I asked somebody what time the production meeting was. They answered "What's a production meeting?"

That's not how you properly prepare for a successful show; matter of fact, that is simply uncontrolled chaos! Meanwhile, Eric would always tell you about planning and plotting out six-month arcs, putting together a "Wrestling Bible" which would detail and describe every wrester on the roster, and all these bullshit buzzwords that his Hollywood buddy Jason Hervey taught him . . . but he never did any of that. He just used the lingo to convince the network execs that he actually had a clue what he was talking about. And, to his credit, they bought it. Shows you how easily they could be worked.

As CM Punk would say, "Tell me when I'm lying." If Easy E knew so much about television, then what happened to the production company he started with Jason: Bischoff Hervey Entertainment? How'd that work out? Outside of *Scott Baio Is 46 . . . and Pregnant*, what did they ever produce that "revolutionized" the television industry? *I Want to Be a Hilton*?!

Man, here I go again. You've unleashed my inner beast as it relates to Eric. But man, he was just so full of shit. It was all smoke and mirrors. It was all talk, it was never about doing the actual work and producing. Eric couldn't write a wrestling show, and to this day he's never written one. But he sure as hell could tell Dixie, Brad, Kevin Kaye, and whoever else was gullible enough how to do it. Rather than "educating" them with your pompous word salad, Eric, how about *showing* them . . . which you never did. Put your money where your mouth is.

There are thousands of wrestling shows created from 1996 through 2012 with my name all over them—every word on those pages was from my pencil. Eric has never gone through that exercise—not even once. And I think, at the end of the day, both Dixie and Brad knew that. They knew that they needed someone to actually do the grunt work—and that that someone was me.

Now, often when I go off on this rant, I always end it with this: Eric Bischoff was neither creative nor a writer; executive, yes, but not a creative writer. And that is fine—we can't all be everything. Each one of us has our strengths and weaknesses. Unfortunately, Eric thought he excelled at everything—and he just didn't. The proof is in his creative at WCW. Yeah, give him credit for the nWo, even though many will tell you he stole the idea from a Japanese promotion, but regardless, the problem was that he would eventually run out of ideas to fuel nWo, which watered the once fearsome threesome down to boring fodder. That creative fail opened the door for the Attitude Era.

Anyway, what Eric excelled at, I sucked at. During my lifetime I've had *two* video stores, a "CD Warehouse," and a pretzel franchise go out of business. That would be 0 for 4 if you're doing the math. I absolutely suck at business. I suck at Executive Board Meetings and making Corporate Business Decisions. Check off all the boxes: suck, suck, suck, and suck.

However, when it comes to structure, discipline, drive, hard work, creativity, and entertainment—I'm your guy. There was a point at TNA, prior to Eric and Hulk coming aboard, where Dixie wanted to offer me a contract that would expand my duties. There was much more money *and* responsibility involved. I politely turned that down—which Dixie didn't accept well—because, as I put it, "I don't want to be anybody's BOSS." I'm not a boss type of guy—I am in the creative lane.

Eric was a boss. Eric wanted to be a boss. Eric wanted power. Eric wanted to be in control. Eric wanted the ability to tell people what to do. Eric loved being FEARED. I carry none of those traits.

Disclaimer

(Please read the disclaimer!)

> I want this to go on the record, and I want to be clear about this. I have been as apologetic as I possibly can be as I've been cutting now 18 chapters of promos on Eric. This was not my intention going in, but by the same token—I refuse to edit myself. You are reading 25 years of built-up anger, animosity, frustration, and at times even borderline hate. That is all my truth. I am not trying to convince you of anything. If you're reading this and you believe Eric is wearing the white hat and villain Vince is full of shit—that is your right and prerogative.

Let me be clear, Eric is not the only person I didn't like in the wrestling business. Here's the list:

- Eric Bischoff
- Paul Heyman
- Jim Cornette

That's it.

When you look at those three names, Bischoff, Heyman, Cornette, what do you see? You see three guys who are synonymous with professional wrestling. To me, they represent everything the business is, what's wrong with it and what I loathe about it the most. And, in not having a high opinion of the wrestling business in general, it's easy to understand why these are not my favorite people.

This is what I've learned in the 13 years since I've been inactive in professional wrestling. The people you see onscreen and behind the scenes are really the people they appear to be. They are people who over the years have transformed inside the wrestling bubble into what they are "supposed to be" and what they are "supposed to represent" while associated with the business. In other words, the Cornettes, the Heymans, the Bischoffs—who you see are who they've really become. They are not simply characters in a fictional business, but they actually have *become* their characters, even once *outside* of the fictive world. For example, all you have to do is listen to, or watch, a Jim Cornette or Eric Bischoff podcast and you will see for yourself. They remain the same exact guys they were since they exited the business.

How do I know this? I watched Eric interact with his son, Garett: he was a great dad. I witnessed conversations with his daughter and wife: father and husband of the year. When Cornette lets his "I'm gonna piss on Vince Russo's grave" guard down, when you see the picture his better half paints on social media—you see Jim chasing his puppy around in a field of lilies and lilacs!!!

In other words—IT'S THE BUSINESS that does it to them. It's the business which hardens their soul. The money, the power, the greed, the ego, all of it has an effect on whom they BECOME—not only when inside the bubble, but also when they leave it.

I witnessed this firsthand when I was active in the business. While everybody was down at the bar slipping mickies and snorting God knows what, I was alone in my hotel room looking myself in a mirror many a night. "Who are you . . . and what have you become?" is a question I asked daily. Man, you don't even realize it. It just overtakes your very being like you would see in all those horror movies where some "Thing" would ingest your entire soul. Remember poor, sweet, little Regan in *The Exorcist*? THAT's what I'm talking about.

So—take the wrestling business away, and you can potentially see different people. I'm reading now how Eric Bischoff has become a mortgage loan officer because he wants to "help people." I believe that. Maybe in his actual heart he does, but will the Eric Bischoff *character* allow him to do this? One would think that the longer you are away from spending the majority of your time in the business, the better a human being you become, but . . . they never allow themselves to be away from the business. That is who they are and what they know.

These are the things that people in the business just don't talk about . . . and they need to. If you have hopes, dreams, and aspirations of getting into wrestling, you really need to know what you are hoping for. The reality is that wrestling *allows* bad behavior. There is no human resources department to keep bad behavior in check. Unless there is a Vince McMahon running the ship, you can literally get away with murder . . . and I mean actual murder. There are no rules, no regulations, and no punishments when your behavior is toxic. And the reason for that is simple: the boys are governing the boys.

There was a case in WCW where a good friend of mine by the name of Christine Johnson, the best senior producer I ever worked with, was sexually harassed by a wrestler/agent on the job. Christine's boss at the time, Keith Mitchell, another superhero of mine, wouldn't stand for it and filed a complaint concerning that individual. When Keith and Christine showed up at the "hearing," those present—who would be weighing the allegations and deciding the fate of the accused—were all peers of the individual charged, with many being ex-wrestlers and all being men.

That's how the shit works in wrestling. You would never get away with the politics, backstabbing, and underhandedness if you worked in any other industry . . . maybe besides the music industry and Hollywood. Think about it, if you took the two greatest politicians in the wrestling business, Eric Bischoff and Paul Heyman, how would they have fared in "normal" jobs? Would Bischoff have lasted as a high school teacher, or Heyman as a bank manager? Think about that. They wouldn't have lasted one day working in the "real" world. The wrestling business allows bad behavior, and, to make matters even worse, bad behavior usually wins.

For the record, I have never alluded to Jim Cornette as a politician because he's not. Maybe it's because he's not smart enough, or maybe he just doesn't want to play the game. When Jim has something to say, he's going to say it. He's never going to edit his words or look around to see who's taking note. He's just going to lash out, like the time he did with WWE's executive producer Kevin Dunn's . . . overbite. Jim referred to Kevin as "Bucky Beaver" in front of everybody in the room. Something you just don't do, but Jim did, and he got away with it. Read the prior paragraph. Think about Jim Cornette in any role outside of wrestling: a delivery person for Amazon, a manager at Walmart, a barista at Starbucks . . . think about what that would look like. Think about what might happen if Jim were to have to live among "normal" people in a "normal" word. Man, would that make the hottest reality show since *Scott Baio Is 46 . . . and Pregnant*, or what?

My point? The wrestling business is a world within itself. There is nothing else like it . . . nothing. Half of those employed in the wrestling business couldn't hold a job in any other industry. Their attitude and behavior would just not be allowed or tolerated. It is the Island of Misfit Toys, and if you ain't one of them . . . it's only a matter of time.

19 ERIC WAS HULK'S PUPPET

Aside from Hulk and Eric making their own rules and their own schedules, the next part of their comedy act that would eventually wear me down was when Eric, Ed, Matt, and I would agree on a talent and a direction, only for Eric to go back to Hulk and get that godforsaken phrase, "That doesn't work for me, brother!" Who cares if it doesn't work for you? You have creative control over *your* creative and nobody else's . . . or . . . did he?

Is it possible that Dixie Carter gave Hulk Hogan the final say over *all* the creative? As far-fetched as that sounds, I had to consider it a possibility at the time because Dixie went along with EVERYTHING Hulk said. I can clearly remember, when Dean Broadhead, the chief financial officer of the company, asked me if TNA should give Hulk creative control. I told Dean that hiring Hulk was one thing, but giving him creative control was something totally different. I explained the headache I had at WCW, and advised Dean against it. It was literally days later that Dean came back and informed me that they did indeed give Hulk Hogan creative control.

Even as I'm typing this I'm asking: Was it TOTAL creative control? That thought never even crossed my mind because nobody could have been that inept. But . . . was Dixie willing to give Hulk whatever he wanted to get him to sign on the dotted line?

The only reason I don't think this was the case was because if it were indeed true . . . I'm sure that Easy E would have thrown it in our faces. Regardless, Hulk always got the final say, and there was no arguing or debating it. Looking back, should I have been the one to stand up to him? The answer is yes, but the reality was that Dixie was never going to take my side over Hulk's. She was such a mark for him that if he had suggested we put the belt on *him* at that time, she would have gone along for the ride.

Some of the things Hulk changed at the last minute weren't worth arguing over, but there were a couple of big beats in the storyline that changed the direction of the entire company. The first one came when we all agreed in a creative meeting to put the TNA World Title on "The Pope" D'Angelo Dinero. Perhaps there is no other talent that I ever worked with who oozed more charisma than Elijah Burke. He just had it. He was dripping in it . . . soaking in it. There was a big PPV coming up that weekend and after much discussion, Matt, Ed, Eric, and I all agreed simultaneously that the belt should be put on the Pope. It was a done deal. So much so that I called Elijah myself, who then contacted all of his family members so they could make arrangements to be at the show for his historical, monumental moment.

Soon thereafter, Eric would inform us, "this doesn't work for Hulk, brother," so we had to come up with a plan B. I have to tell you, I never argued with Eric because I knew that if I did it would turn out bad . . . real bad . . . and I did everything in my power to prevent that from happening.

Eric never once overruled his "best bud" Hulk. Again, I wouldn't find out their working agreement until literally about a month ago, when Eric explained he never wanted to go to TNA but did just because "Hulk wanted him to."

So, guess who was the one who had to go back to the talent and tell them there was a "change in plans"? Not Eric. Yeah, it absolutely sucked having to tell Elijah that we decided to go in "another direction." I hate that !@#$%^& phrase. That !@#$%^& phrase means only one thing: politics.

When this story came out, there were some who accused Hulk of being a racist, and that was the reason for him denying Elijah. I don't believe that for a minute. I never saw any racist qualities in Hulk. Back in the day it was clear, if Hulk thought he could make money with you, he was going to do business with you, black, white, yellow, or green. The true reason he put the kibosh on Elijah? Well, instead of the Pope, it was Hulk's Favorite Son . . . RVD.

Man, this was bullshit. It was all bullshit. Whatever "pact" that Hulk and Eric had, Dixie was paying Eric's paycheck, so his loyalty should have been with her. But it wasn't—it never was. It was never about what was best for business; it was about what was best for Hulk. I hope you're really starting to see the picture here. This is what we were up against, with zero backing from the boss, Dixie.

STREAM OF CONSCIOUSNESS

JUST ADDED!!!

I wrote that prior paragraph two days ago. Today, I read these comments from Bret Hart:

> The truth is that in the end, I remember that day when [Hogan] was trying to change it or cancel it or ruin the whole idea, Eric Bischoff . . . he doesn't really know what the hell he's doing, he never ever did. But I remember he could never do anything and told me I had to get everything approved through Hulk Hogan. And that tells me that Hulk Hogan was the boss over Eric Bischoff and Bischoff was just a front man for Hogan. Between the two of them, they killed WCW. You can put it right on Hogan or Eric Bischoff. They're both accountable.

So, there it is: Bret Hart had the exact same sentiments years earlier when it came to the "puppet" and the "puppeteer" at WCW. This was the play, the act, the work.

I guess Bret is a Pathological Liar too.

I remember getting to the point of loathing those meetings with Eric. They made me physically ill. Yes—physically. I can remember one session where I was feeling a bit feverish, under the weather, so I went to the bathroom just to take a breather only to find out my body was breaking out in hives. BRO—!@#$%^& HIVES! Eric Bischoff gave me *hives*! I had never gotten them before, or since.

But the Pope was just the beginning. The bigger hit would soon follow.

Perhaps the most respectful human being I have ever met, let alone worked with, was Bobby Roode. As a head writer, if I'd had a roster full of Bobby Roodes, I would have had a billion-dollar company. Bobby was just everything you wanted a wrestler and human being to be. He was special. There aren't enough words in the dictionary to describe how I felt about Bobby. He was a Pro's Pro and a Man's Man.

Bobby Roode's time had come in TNA. Everybody knew it. He worked his way through the ranks and became a company favorite both in front of the camera and behind the curtain. Everybody was rooting for Bobby—everybody. So the decision to put him over Kurt Angle to become the new TNA champion was an easy one. Kurt couldn't wait to put Bobby over. He was eager to pass the torch to a new generation that would carry it with honor, integrity, pride, respect, and class.

I remember the night before, me and Matt Conway took Bobby Roode out to dinner, and Bobby was so excited about it. He worked so hard for this opportunity. Like the Pope, Bobby had also invited his entire family to the show for this once-in-a-lifetime event that was to take place in less than 24 hours.

There was much excitement in the air in the production meeting that day. Man, everybody was just a fan of Bobby's, not one person had anything bad to say about him, and trust me—that is rare in the pro wrestling business. That morning, as we go into the production meeting, Hulk takes a seat next to Dixie.

Uh-oh.

Out of nowhere, literally hours before the show, Hulk brings up "WHAT IF" Bobby Roode does not win the title? Me and Conway look at each other. Now? You're going to bring this up NOW? This had been the plan for weeks. The TV shows leading up to this were written to build up this moment. Dixie just sat there. You could see her turn a little red in the face because even she wanted Bobby to get his just fruits. But . . . she said nothing. She sat there and said nothing.

Was this a rib? Was the Hulk/Bischoff Show just a bad rib on all of us? Was Hulk effing things up just because he could? None of this made any sense to anybody, but again, nobody was going to say anything.

This I regret. If anybody, I should have stood up for Bobby, no matter what the consequences. It's not that I was afraid of being fired; I just knew that if my Italian Temper went off . . . it wasn't going to be good for anybody.

Needless to say, Bobby Roode didn't win the TNA World Title that night. But what did come out of it was that I was pushed to the brink. The next Pope/Bobby Roode Incident . . . would be the last of its kind.

20 A SWING AND A MISS

When you are writing one show, sometimes two, plus a pay-per-view every month—there are going to be some clunkers. Nobody is going to have a hundred-percent no-dud rate. That is not improbable, it's impossible. In an earlier chapter, I came up with some of my own personal misses; but in this chapter, I'm going to lay out three of the greatest fails to come out of the Hogan/Bischoff Regime.

1. ABYSS'S "MAGIC" RING

This brainchild was Hulk's baby from the jump. Somehow, some way, Hulk's WWE Hall of Fame ring became a magical, mystical stone that controlled the monster Abyss. Seriously—don't even ask me why, or how, but Hulk loved this idea. And Abyss (Chris Park) rolled with it like the pro he was, but man, this went nowhere. An absolute swing and a miss from the red and yellow.

2. AJ STYLES AS RIC FLAIR JR.

I'm going to write this off as a rib on AJ because—was it bad. Hulk and Eric actually wanted AJ Styles to *bleach his hair* and dress in sequinned robes like the Nature Boy himself. There was ZERO logic to this, and to AJ's credit he said a big, fat no thank you!!!

3. SAMOA JOE GETS KIDNAPPED

You almost had to be witness to this pitch to understand—Matt Conway, Ed, and I were. Eric pitched that Samoa Joe would be kidnapped by a band of ninjas and thrown in the back of a white van. The payoff was that Jimmy "Superfly" Snuka was behind the kidnapping, who Eric swore he could get. We all thought this was the drizzling shits, but in an effort to try and support Eric for the sake of trying to get along with him—we agreed to do it. But let's be clear about one thing—this was Eric's baby, one hundred percent.

When it came time to produce the pre-tape, Eric was nowhere to be found. So the ninjas threw Samoa Joe into a white van, only for Eric to come back the next week and tell us he couldn't get Superfly Snuka.

Years later, Samoa Joe would bury me in an interview. I didn't have Joe's number, but I had his email address, so I wrote him saying "I listened to your interview. Is there something I need to apologize for? I did not know you felt that way about me. Smarten me up because if I was wrong about something, I will apologize for it."

Joe went on to write me this long, long, long email, the gist of it being, "Vince, when you creatively had me kidnapped, thrown in a white van, and taken away, that story never went anywhere. When you did that, you killed my career!"

Being that I was in the trenches and working with him on that scene and because I was the one producing it, Joe assumed that it had been my idea. As bad as I thought the idea was, never did I throw Eric under the bus. Never did I say to Joe—and Joe didn't like it at the time either—"This ain't my idea—this is freaking Eric's!" So, for years Joe went on carrying this grudge against me that revolved around an idea that was never mine.

After I got Joe's reply, I told him that all of that was on Eric Bischoff, and if he didn't believe me, he should have a conversation with Matt Conway, who was still working with the company.

21 ERIC FELICIANO

In the vein of being fair, there was one particular piece Eric came up with that I absolutely loved. Eric wanted to open a show with him sitting in the middle of the ring with a bright white spotlight glaring down on him, as he strummed away on an acoustic guitar with the mastery of José Feliciano. Eric did such a great job on this open that to this day people still believe he was actually playing.

As you can see, I didn't put over many of Eric's ideas, nor did I bury dozens. Why—because he simply didn't come up with ideas. As I said earlier in the book, it was just not his forte. Now, like Vince, you could give him a complete show, and he could redline the shit out of it with the best of them, but to come up with a show from scratch—that would have been the equivalent of me being in charge of talent relations and all those WCW millionaires—man, would that have been a disaster.

22 ERIC THE TALENT

While I point out that we can't all be good at everything, we clearly all have our gifts. One of Eric's greatest attributes was that he was an outstanding in-ring performer. With Hogan, Hall, and Nash, three Wrestling Icons, Eric rarely gets the credit he deserves. Without Eric, I don't believe that the "feel" would have been the same—he played a huge part in the nWo. As the front-man of the most dominant group in wrestling history, Eric stole the show practically every week. Eric always had a great television presence; dare I say, in the role of the authority figure, nobody has done it with more conviction than Eric except perhaps Vince McMahon himself.

And, speaking of Vince, one of my pitches to him when I almost re-signed with the WWE in 2002 was to bring in Eric as an on-air character. Now you may be thinking that was a no-brainer, but at that time Eric had never worked for the WWE, and the possibility of it ever happening was slim at best.

But that's where I differ from many, especially in the wrestling business. If I felt you could help the company that I was working for, I was going to suggest that you become a part of it. I always felt my responsibility was to the person paying me—and regardless how I felt about Eric personally . . . in an on-air role, he could help the company.

Eric, in my opinion, never got the props for his flair for the dramatic, simply because he was in the shadow of "Mr. McMahon." Nobody was ever going to top that character—I don't care who you were—but if Vince hadn't existed in that role, perhaps people would still be talking about "nWo Eric" today instead.

I'm fair, man, and I give my props. I give all the credit in the world . . . where it is due. Eric just excelled in some positions over others, but in wrestling, the more you pushed what you *thought* you could do, the more power you would receive. And that's what it all comes down to. You criss-cross lanes, and tread in areas that you may not excel in, simply to become more powerful to the boys. That's the one thing you never had at the WWF when I worked there.

Myself, JR, Kevin Dunn, and every other top executive all had roles. You got paid to do one specific job and you never floated over to others. JR never crossed the line into creative, and I rarely, unless contacted by a talent, ever stuck my nose in talent relations. I would have been horrible in that job, so why would I ever go anywhere near it? The same with Kevin Dunn over on the TV side, Kevin never got involved in the creative process regardless of what the dirt sheets have reported.

Vince believed in structure; we all knew what our roles were. TNA, under Dixie Carter, never had that same structure, not even close. This allowed Eric Bischoff to get involved in every aspect of the business, whether it was his forte or not. If he would have just stuck to the business end of TV, handling Hulk and killing it as an onscreen character—there would have never been an issue. However, when you insert yourself elsewhere, in positions where you think you excel but you don't . . . that's where many of the issues began.

23 DIXIE THE TALENT

Aside from my Eric issues mounting, there were also some memorable things happening at TNA at the time.

One fine day, just out of the blue, I got a call from Dixie's closest associate at TNA. It was a gentleman who had worked closely with Dixie at the PR company she owned prior to her wrestling venture. Once she took over TNA, he continued on as her righthand man. Let's call him Andy.

"What do you think about Dixie Carter being an on-air character?" Andy asked when I picked up the phone.

At that time it was just me and Matt Conway doing the writing. Ed had exited the company because Dixie no longer had use for him and surely could no longer afford to pay him due to the expense of the Hulk/Eric contracts. I didn't even fight it, I knew Ed wasn't depending on the job, had the talent to be successful at whatever he chose and because of the current situation—and I knew he wasn't thrilled to be there in the first place!

I said to Matt, "This has Dixie's name written all over it." Why would Andy, whom we *never* heard from creatively, just pull this idea out of thin air? And, knowing Dixie as well as I did, I knew she would never come up to us and say, "Write me on TV." No, she would have someone else do it.

My stance on this was simple: Dixie owns this company, and if she wants to be on TV, then put her on TV. I just wish she had felt secure enough about herself and the idea to tell us directly. As a writer, I was always confident in my ability to get anybody over. Of course, you had to have some charisma—the "It Factor" does help—but good writing could make anybody interesting.

And I'm not saying Dixie wasn't interesting, she was. Attractive Business Woman from a Wealthy Family running a Wrestling Company—there's a lot of meat on that bone. My only concern came from a producing standpoint. Let me explain.

As I touched upon earlier, when we were at Universal Studios in Orlando, the female talent used to arrive first because they had to get hair and makeup so they would be ready for pre-tapes once the production meeting broke.

"Get your hair and makeup so when I come back we can get started," I always barked.

When the meeting ended 90 minutes later, I would march directly to the makeup room, ready to go, only to see a line of Knockouts waiting on hair and makeup while Dixie Carter sat in the chair, relaxed and texting on her phone. Keep in mind, this was *before* she was on TV. Man, if the TNA Knockouts' looks could kill, she'd have been one expired CEO!

So now you have to imagine—what might Dixie's behavior be if she were a character on TV?! No doubt she was going to be high-maintenance; I'm talking Kardashian-style high-maintenance! No way I was going to be able to produce her like I would another talent; I knew she was going to demand much of my time.

That's what was running through my mind. Never at any time did I oppose her being a TV character, I just knew—based on experience—it was going to be timely. The way Dixie worked was that she would never just come out and tell you what she was thinking or wanted, she would just keep dropping hint after hint until you finally figured it out and did it. There was no time for that on a TV day. At Universal, there were days I would shoot 30 pre-tapes—there was no wiggle room in there to kowtow to one talent, but in this case the talent would be my boss.

Let me take a quick left here. When people ask me who was the easiest talent to produce, without even putting a second of thought to it I answer Vince McMahon. When I was ready to shoot with Vince, I would tell him what I needed and he would do exactly what I asked. He never questioned anything and never wasted a second of my time. Why? Because Vince understood my workload; he knew there were dozens of talents that I needed to tend to, and the less time I spent with him, the more I had for the Austins, the Rocks, and the Takers. Dixie either didn't understand that or didn't care. Everything was a million questions being hashed over and over again.

But if I thought it was a bad idea for Dixie to be on camera, I would have told her. I think Eric once suggested in an interview that I was trying to "work" him by telling him, "You know this is really a bad idea—you need to tell Dixie." That is all BULLSHIT. If I had an issue, I would have told her myself; but I knew she was an attractive woman, and I knew she would have a presence on television. I also realized that the possibilities with that character could be endless, but I also understood the reality—it was going to be extremely time-consuming.

As a character, Dixie was tremendous. Everybody hates their rich boss, especially if she's a Southern Belle with a silver spoon hanging out the side of her mouth. She generated a ton of heat, something many seasoned veteran heels can't even garner in 2025. I never regretted writing her in for one second, but my experience working with her in that capacity was everything I thought it would be.

24 WHERE IS DOUBLE J IN ALL THIS?

I'd literally need the confines of a psychiatrist's couch for about six or seven days to explain my very complicated relationship with "Double J" Jeff Jarrett. It was probably '94 or '95 when I first met Jeff in my role as editor of *WWF Magazine*. One of the earliest times we spent together was when Jeff, Shane McMahon, and I went to Vegas to get content for both the magazine and TV. I remember we shot some footage with Jeff and comedian Rip Taylor (look him up—guy was a full-fledged WACKO) and various celebrity impersonators. Even though I hardly ever drink, I do remember getting a little tipsy one night and feeling embarrassed because I caught both Shane and Jeff rolling their eyes at me. I was young, what can I tell ya?

Over the years, Jeff and I developed a bond. I always viewed Jeff as different from the other wrestlers. Looking back, I really do believe it was that Southern Charm. Coming from the mean streets of Long Island, you were just not used to people being kind, nice, and polite. Man, Jeff's smile could light up the Midtown Tunnel, and that laugh was just so infectious.

I'd be lying if I said I wasn't shocked when Jeff left the WWF in the middle of the night. It was in the midst of a storyline with his roadie, "The Road Dogg" Jesse James (Brian James), where Double J was going to be exposed for staking claim for singing "With My Baby Tonight" when in fact it was Brian who was the crooner. Jeff never smartened me up to his leaving; the only thing I remember was that he and Brian were in a hurry to get out of the building that night.

Jeff would eventually go to WCW and then come back to the WWF where I was in a more prominent position on the card as the head writer of TV. Jeff and I picked up right where we left off. He was the closest thing I had to a friend when it came to the boys.

Week after week, I would find something special for Jeff to do on *Raw* . . . if I'm going to be totally honest with you, Vince never saw Jeff as a "top guy," mainly because of his size. But even though he was my friend, I also thought Jeff had enormous talent.

Jeff was an old school heel, a character that could get instant heat on himself while shining the babyface—to him it was like brushing his teeth. And, man, could he go. You always hear about what a great technician Bret Hart was in the ring—and he was, but he had nothing on Jeff. Jeff was so technically sound, like a machine—crisp, clean, and with impact. And, perhaps the most important element of Jeff's game—he never got hurt. You could depend on him to be there and ready to go one hundred percent of the time.

During the Attitude Era, Jeff and I got even closer. I guess you can say as close as you can get to a wrestler, anyway. It was at Owen Hart's funeral where I met Jeff's beautiful and lovely wife, Jill. Man, Jill was an absolute Saint of a Woman. What a gift from God. Jill and Jeff were just the perfect match, high school sweethearts with three adorable fair-haired young girls.

When I made the move to WCW, Jeff found his way back over. I was thrilled to have him. Who wouldn't want a dozen Jeff Jarretts on their roster? I put all my eggs in the Jeff Jarrett Basket, with many accusing me of favoritism. BULL. SHIT. I put Jeff in that spot because he earned it, deserved it, and I could both count on and most importantly trust him. And he never let me down. Not one, single time.

I cover the early history between me and Jeff, and the origin of TNA, in my second book, *Rope Opera: How WCW Killed Vince Russo*. I carried the story through Jeff being sent home by Dixie due to his relationship with Karen Angle. Jeff was expelled prior to Eric and Hulk joining the company. Once Eric and Hulk came in, I was constantly trying to find ways to work Jeff back into the fold. Unfortunately, I think he thought the opposite. I think he thought I was trying to keep him out. That notion was absolutely ridiculous. Jeff was my friend; Eric and Hulk were far from buds. But that's just the paranoid side of professional wrestling that is forever prevalent. I was trying to get Jeff back in the mix, but I knew it was going to take time. He had lost a lot of trust over the Karen situation, and Dixie needed some time to get over it.

Man, Jeff was in a really bad place at that time, but I totally understood why. Even though he may have brought the situation onto himself, he had to feel like a guy that had his own company, his baby, taken away from him not once, but twice—first Dixie, then Eric and Hulk. And in a way . . . he was right.

I was slowly, but surely, able to work Jeff back into some storylines. The scenario was that he was doing menial labor in an effort to get back into Eric's good graces. Man, was fiction mirroring reality. Jeff didn't like Eric, and Eric gladly returned the favor. Eric tried to keep Jeff as far away as possible, seeing him as a threat to his "power."

I would always smarten Jeff up to Eric's business plans because I valued Jeff's opinion and wanted to hear his thoughts. Right around this time, Eric was politicking that *Impact* needed to go live every week. Jeff thought that would be a financial nightmare. I was able to convince Eric to hear Jeff out, and he did, only arguing with everything Jeff said.

TNA would eventually try going live every week, and it was just another Eric failure, much like the head-to-head war with the WWE. Man, you're not right all the time, even though Eric usually believed he was.

This was turning into an absolute MESS! These personalities were just not meshing. So what did Dixie do . . . ? Well, hell, let's just add another layer.

25 CALLING BROTHER LOVE

A few chapters back, I was talking about Jim Cornette and his "foundational" hatred towards me simply because to him I was, am, and always will be a "yankee from the east." Jim use to always refer to me as a yankee, thinking that was a derogatory word and it would piss me off. I always had to remind Jim that we actually had a baseball team *named the Yankees*, so the word wasn't insulting at all.

I think those from the South may actually have the reverse effect on me. As I spoke about the "Southern Charm" of Jeff Jarrett in the previous chapter, it pales in comparison to the "Texas twang" of Bruce Prichard.

I have known Bruce for some 30 years now, and even though our relationship can be referred to as "rocky" at best, I can tell you that I have never met a person with more charm and charisma than Bruce Prichard. When I think of Bruce, I think of a happy-go-lucky, jovial man, much like John Candy or Chris Farley. And, on the surface, Bruce is really a kind soul, coming across as a friend and somebody who really cares about your well-being.

But . . . be aware . . . we are talking about the wrestling business here.

To really get down to the point, Bruce fits the cliché of being a wolf in sheep's clothing the way Cardi B fits into her snug spandex pants—tight and comfortable. The wool is tight, white, and soft, but deep within lies a beast who will rip your heart out, chew on it a bit, then proceed to spit it out if it means his political gain. And Bruce was such a pro at this, you never saw it coming and only realized it when it was too late.

Initially, when I worked with Bruce in the WWF, I was one of the ones who never saw it coming. As a matter of fact, I even considered him my friend. Bruce would have my wife and kids to his house for barbeques, and on one occasion Amy and I went out with him and his wife, Stephanie, to see *Grease* on Broadway for her birthday—with Bruce footing the bill for all . . . while also getting Amy plastered, by the way—but that was Bruce. If you were going to go out with him, it was going to be a good time.

To this day, I still consider Bruce, along with the late, great Jack "Blackjack" Lanza, as my mentor, with "Cowboy" Bill Watts giving me my big break (all that is documented in *Forgiven*). When I was just the lowly editor of *WWF Magazine*, Bruce would bring me on video shoots. One very memorable one involved a graveyard, the middle of the night, and the Undertaker and Paul Bearer. Back then, I really envied Bruce. I looked up to him, I respected him. Nobody had the relationship with Vince that Bruce had; even though at the time I never quite understood it, I always admired and respected it. Why? Because I knew that relationship meant everything to Bruce.

Bruce was the best producer I ever worked with by far—there is nobody that even comes a close second. On my best day, Bruce could produce circles around me. The gift that Bruce had, which I didn't, was that he was a great performer (google "Brother Love") and could slip into every character as he produced them! That was amazing—an absolute gift.

It's funny, because as I sit here and I write this . . . I'm smiling. I miss Bruce. I miss our conversations. I miss working with him. I don't have any ill will towards him whatsoever, but, as he looks back now, and I'm sure Vince McMahon feels the same, Vince Russo was just a guy they worked with 25 to 30 years ago—another vessel that sailed through the sea of the business, here today and gone tomorrow. And that hurts, because those relationships I had back then meant something to me . . . and they still do.

With Bruce, back in my WWF heyday, it was keep your friends close and your enemies closer. The story of how he betrayed me—the first time—is also well documented in *Forgiven*. The second time, I saw it coming. My eyes were open, and I expected it. The only one I have to blame is myself.

Every wrestling mark carrying a belt over their shoulder at a house show or doing a podcast trying to put themselves over as an "insider" understands how difficult and almost impossible it is to get a job in the wrestling business. With few limited spots, unless you stand out and are far superior to the other marks, you're probably going to be doing a show in your momma's basement with a fluorescent pink sign hanging over your head. However, what's perhaps even more impossible than landing a job with a major wrestling promotion is getting back in after you've been fired.

That was the case with Bruce after he had been terminated by the WWE. Even though he had been Vince's righthand man for decades, when daughter Stephanie came into power, Brother Love lost his shine with the boss. Remember I told you that Triple H and Stephanie did everything to try and reverse Vince's decision after he rehired me without their knowledge in 2002? Well, Bruce experienced the same wrath a few years later.

In wrestling, when you're in a position of power, you just don't want anybody around who could be a threat to your throne. And Bruce was a threat to the "Power Couple" because he had more creative knowledge in his pinky toe than the two of them had combined.

Bruce loved wrestling, what else was he going to do, become a plumber like his infamous creation TL Hopper?! (I had to get that dig in, sorry.) As I stated earlier, Bruce is one of those guys that just can't exist without pro wrestling. Now, years later, Bruce would make a living as a podcaster due to the fact that he's the greatest storyteller in the history of the business, but back then there was no such thing as podcasting.

So, Bruce reached out to me, via phone call, poking around, but—let me be clear—never asking for a job. However, he didn't need to . . . I understood his position.

Man, I will give you this advice until I no longer have the strength to type the words on a page: don't ever forget those who helped you get to where you are—ever. It has happened to me over and over and over again, with the Matt Conways and Jeremy Borashes of the world. I literally took these guys under my wing, taught them everything they know about TV, writing, and producing, and today . . . not even a !@#$%^& Christmas card. I never forget those who created and paved that road for me, whether it be "Fast" Eddie Ferrara, Jack Lanza, Ed Ricciuti (my first editor at *WWF Magazine*), the late, great Louie Gianfriddo (the assistant editor of the magazine), or Bruce Prichard.

I was indebted to Bruce; I owed Bruce. Add to that his wife, Stephanie, who was dealing with cancer at the time, and the two kids who were dependent on him. I knew I had to do the right thing, even though I knew exactly what Bruce's game would be if he ever got his foot in the TNA door. Man, if Bruce would have just come in and done what I needed him to do, that would have made my life so much easier . . . but I knew from the start that wasn't going to be the case.

Honestly, I wouldn't have tried to shoehorn Bruce in if there wasn't a need—I absolutely didn't want Dixie to spend more money that I knew she didn't have—but at the time Ed was already gone from the company, and the pre-tape schedule at TV was just overwhelming. Sometimes we would record six or eight shows over two days, and there just weren't enough hours in the day for me to get all those pre-tapes in the can, even if I worked 7 a.m. to 11p.m. And, no, I was never going to cut down on my own workload. Remember?—I don't settle for mediocrity.

So, again, despite knowing what the outcome would be, I went to Dixie and pitched a role for Bruce, to at least secure him a weekly paycheck. I created a spot for Bruce where he would just go to TVs as a producer, so Dixie wouldn't have to pay him an exorbitant amount of money. That was the key; I knew she couldn't afford to pay him a hefty salary. Dixie bit—Bruce got the job, and he was very appreciative. Man, I was thrilled for him, Bruce needs the wrestling business in his life, and without it . . . he's just not whole.

But . . . Bruce didn't waste one single second.

Here's the game, you turn around and you catch them in conversation. They know what they're doing. They look the other way, hoping you didn't notice, but—you did. It happened with J.J. Dillon and Kevin Sullivan, and now history was repeating itself with the constant sidebars between Dixie and Bruce.

Bro, I swear to you, I didn't get upset, I didn't get angry . . . I knew it was coming.

26 DIXIE'S DILEMMA

It's always been amazing to me the way God works. You never *exactly* know what he's doing, or why he's doing it, but you know that destiny, his Divine Hand, is slowly, softly, gently, quietly—and sometimes chaotically—putting things in place.

Ironically, right around the same time that Bruce is working the britches off an unsuspecting Dixie, the heat is building up on a daily basis between Eric and me. The two of us were at the point of not agreeing on anything. With the situation about to become toxic, Dixie makes the decision that when there is a difference of opinion between Eric and me creatively . . . she was going to make the final call.

Bro . . .

Are you !@#$%^& kidding me? Dixie couldn't decide what color eye shadow to wear on TV; you think she's going to be the special referee between me and Eric?! That just wasn't going to happen. So, of course, it was only a matter of days before Dixie had to make her first call. And, as easy as it was to predict—she hid in her office like a shivering, shaking dog hides from thunder. She wasn't making any decisions. She never did, and you really think she was going to start now?!

Listen, I, at times, consider myself a Great Writer, but no way, no how could I have scripted this shiznit.

STREAM OF CONSCIOUSNESS

Man, I'm eating way too many nuts.

About seven months ago I started having some health issues. I was literally peeing every hour, couldn't stop drinking, was losing weight daily without trying to, and no matter how much I drank I constantly had dry mouth. And, oh yeah, one of side of my ballsack was the size of an avocado.

Now, if you know me, you know that I absolutely hate doctors. Look, I don't want to know I'm going to die, I just want to die. Plus, with the world-wide interweb, I can be my own doctor, all I need to do is google my symptoms. So I go online, and type in the above, and the answer is a thousand-percent . . . I have full-blown diabetes. I was always worried about this. My mother was diabetic, and my sister has also had the disease for decades.

At this point, I realize that I need to at least go get a blood test to see what's going on. This alone was going to be a nightmare because every time I have to go to a doctor my blood pressure goes sky high because I get nervous. I know once they put that balloon gimmick on my arm it's going to read like I'm on the verge of a full-blown HEART ATTACK—which it did. I had to ask them to take it over so I could relax myself a bit, which they did and of course it was lower.

A few days later, my results came back. There's one test that's specific for measuring sugar levels in your blood—I forget the letters—anyway, that normal number is around a 6, but my blood read at a 12.4. I knew it; I had skipped right over prediabetes and was a full-fledged diabetic.

The day was January 23, 2024, the day before my birthday. Immediately, the doctor wanted to put me on meds, but I said thanks but no thanks. I don't do meds. With the effects that I've witnessed pills have on wrestlers, I stay as far away from them as possible. I talked the doctor into giving me three months to diet and exercise to see if I could naturally fix the problem—he agreed.

I don't fool around with health, and when I make a commitment to something I always see it through. For the next three months I did weights and cardio daily, along with cutting all sugar and carbs out of my diet—*all* of them—no desserts, pizza, pasta, bread—NONE. Now prior to my symptoms, I was weighing in at about 240 pounds. The swollen nutsack, unnaturally losing the weight, etc., had brought me down to about 225 pounds. After three months, before I went in for my next test, I was at 193—down 32 total pounds. My blood sugar level went from 12.4 to about 6.1. SUCCESS?!

Not quite.

The combination of losing so much weight so fast and constantly drinking coffee to help curb my appetite ballooned my cholesterol, which had been normal on the first test.

Back to the regimen, back for another test in six months.

Helpful Hint: As a complete sugar addict, what gave me my daily sugar "fix" was one short slug of heavy cream before I poured it in my coffee. Try it.

One day, a very memorable day, Matt Conway and I are in the conference room at the TNA offices, slaving away at the creative as we usually were. I was suddenly summoned to Dixie's office. As I hit the door, I see her and Bruce having a conversation inside—I think they were both sitting on a couch.

This is the New Yawk in me. I got it, I got it immediately—nothing had to be said.

But she said it anyway.

"Vince, rather than me, I've decided that Bruce is going to settle whatever creative differences you and Eric have."

Now, you have to remember, at this point Eric and Bruce are BEST BUDS. I guess this developed while they were working together at the WWE. There was little friendship between me and Bruce at the time; it was clear that I was just a vessel to get his large frame through the door at TNA.

She went on: "Going forward, you and Matt will write the show as you usually do" (no shit) "then, you will send the show to Eric. Eric will make his comments on the show and then send them to Bruce. Once Bruce looks at the show, along with Eric's comments, he will then make his own comments. Once he does that, Bruce will send the show back to you and Matt to make the adjustments."

I'm not even going to use these !@#$%^& symbols here—ARE YOU FUCKING KIDDING ME?!

Let me get this straight, the guy who Titanic-ed the ratings at WWF, Bruce Prichard, with Mantaur, TL Hopper, the Goon, Freddie Joe Floyd, Who, etc., who forced Vince McMahon to roll the dice and go in a completely different direction—ME—and the guy I also creatively replaced at WCW because he, too, drove ratings into the ground, Eric Bischoff, are now going to edit MY FUCKING SHOW and tell *me* what to do? No disrespect to Dixie, but was she fucking high?!

Once I'd had a second to digest her total incompetence, having been worked by the "Bobbsey Twins," I came to the realization that what Dixie was in fact telling me was "Bruce Prichard is now your boss."

It took Brother Love two weeks—*two weeks*—to bypass me in a company I had spent almost an entire decade in. As I stated earlier, this is exactly what I expected to happen, but . . . TWO FUCKING WEEKS?!

I sat for a second to take all this in. The look on Bruce's face . . . he couldn't even look his ol' friend Vinnie Ru in the eye. And, perhaps, what was even more ridiculous about Dixie's new plan was the time constraints it put on the writing of the show. Creating, writing, formatting, editing a show every week—you don't have the luxury of time. Were Matt and I supposed to be sitting there with our thumbs up our asses as we waited for Tennessee Tuxedo and his side kick Waldo to redline the shit out of our show?

I'm sorry, and I do love her to this day, but Dixie, unknowing and unsuspecting, was just worked by the best in the business. No way I was going to go along with this plan. If nothing else, I wasn't going to give either Eric or Bruce the satisfaction. Man, I would have loved to be the third party on the phone when Bruce and Eric concocted this scheme, knowing full well that Dixie was going to buy it because it was her out. They had to have been doing more thigh slapping than the Young !@#$%^& Bucks.

This was my Vince "hire a nanny to raise your kids" McMahon moment. I was done. No way I was going to waste my time with this. This was typical Dixie Carter: find somebody else to make my decisions for me because I just can't. The layers that would be added to such a simple process were incomprehensible. The time when wrestling was at its absolute height was when a guy from New York and a guy from New Jersey were doing the writing. Two guys, not three, not six, not a dozen—TWO.

Man, I had gone through this with her so many times before. Who has the "magic wand" to wave around my office and turn this clusterfuck into the WWE? Is it JR? Is it Hulk? Eric? How about Paul !@#$%^& Heyman?

Oh, I didn't tell you about Dixie's total abomination concerning Paul Heyman?

STREAM OF CONSCIOUSNESS

WOW—that's a bunch of f-bombs coming from a Christian guy. And, make no mistake about it, I love Jesus Christ, I am absolutely nothing without him, but these words need to come out of me. These feelings and emotions can no longer be repressed.

I can't tell you how many times, when I go off the rails, people will throw my Christianity in my face. They fail to understand that a) I am human, and b) a foundational part of being Christian is admitting that you are a FLAWED human being, and you can't do this without God's love, patience, understanding, and forgiveness.

So, I have every intention of having a conversation with my Lord and Savior once this book is complete, apologizing for some of the things I may have said . . . but for my own personal well-being and growth—they need to come out.

But, here's the beauty of being a Christian, you are hearing this venom come from my soul because it is bringing me back to a very dark and destructive time of my life. An experience I wish I had never lived but at the same time one I embrace for making me the man I am today. However, I sit here today giving full forgiveness for those who wronged me. There is no hatred inside me whatsoever. I lost the feeling of hate once God moved into my soul.

So, God, yeah, I'm sorry for my language, but it is necessary to my growth.

It's ironic; as I'm writing this book, I watched an interview with Kimberly Page, the former wife of WCW legend Diamond Dallas Page, last night. Kimberly and Dallas Page had an extremely tight relationship with Eric and his wife, Loree.

During the course of the interview, Kimberly stated that she "feared" Eric at work—was actually afraid of him. To paraphrase, she basically said that once he put on his "boss cap" . . . he more or less was a Giant Dick. Kimberly then talked about the "personal" Eric, the friend, the father, the husband, and paints a much different picture of him away from the workplace.

It was only a few pages back where I basically suggested the same exact premise: there were two Erics—there had to be.

So, as Steve Austin would say, the bottom line is that Eric made a conscious decision to be a dick at work, and a dick to those he worked with—one of whom would have been me. Why, man? Why? Why was there such a need to flex your muscles in an effort to display your power and authority as opposed to just being a good human being? Was it just a role you were playing? It seems so, doesn't it? And, if so, then yeah—all these years later, you owe me an apology. You were a dick, and you knew you were a dick.

What I'm saying is that Eric didn't need to be the way he was . . . he chose to be that way.

27 HEYMAN

As I mentioned earlier, I don't love the beloved Paul Heyman as many others seem to. And there are three good reasons for that, which I will present here.

1. POLITICS

There's a reason that people like Bruce and Paul have been around in the wrestling business for as long as they have. Yeah, they need to be smart, talented, and have the knowledge needed in order to have the staying power that they do, but they also need to have the intelligence and the knowhow of "playing the game." "Protecting your spot" is the term they use in the business when you have a knack of keeping those who are better, or have the potential of being better, at arm's length.

Paul did this to Mike Sanders, a very good friend of mine. Mike was a guy I worked with at WCW, who was perhaps the most underrated wrestler and stick man in the history of the biz. Mike had it all: he was athletic, good looking, could both wrestle and act, and he was blessed with the gift of gab. Mike was also probably his own worst enemy, as some may have taken his extreme confidence as utter arrogance. But, though Mike rubbed some the wrong way, he wasn't arrogant—not at all—he was just better.

During the time of the WWE purchase of WCW, Mike was backstage at a WWE TV event. It was there Mike met Paul Heyman for the first time. Heyman was the "Big Dog" on the microphone back then, and Mike felt that Paul saw him as a threat. Just the vibe Sanders received from Heyman made him feel like, "I'm never going to be hired at this place . . . Paul will never allow that to happen."

Needless to say . . . it never happened.

And that's how it works. That's how you protect your spot. If somebody comes along that may be a threat to your throne, you do everything in your power to cockblock that individual.

Paul did that to me when I "almost" went back to the WWE in 2002. After I met with the creative team, it was both Paul and Michael Hayes, the two slimy veterans, who made sure that the entire thing was KIBOSHED. How do I know that? Years later, a few writers in that meeting told me. The funny thing is—they didn't need to. I knew it was going to happen the second I stepped out of the room and Vince stepped in. I was a threat: if Vince hired me to oversee all of TV, there was no need for either one of them.

And, surprise, surprise—almost 25 years later and they are BOTH STILL THERE. Who'd have thunk?

2. HE'S A LIAR

Few people know that Vince McMahon was secretly funding the "outlaw" group ECW during its heyday, and part of the agreement between Vince and Paul was that the two companies would exchange talent. How this would work is simple: If a talent was not getting over in the WWF for whatever reason—maybe they needed more reps, to work in front of more people, character tweak, whatever—we would send them over to ECW to get a bit more seasoning. On the other hand, if I saw an ECW talent on TV that I was interested in, Vince would call Paul, inform him that we want so-and-so, then so-and-so would come over to our side.

This arrangement was laid out directly from Vince McMahon to me.

The first act that I marked out for at ECW were the Dudleys, specifically Bubba and Devon. Back then, Bubba was doing the stuttering gimmick, which I thought was entertaining as all hell. Upon falling in love with Bubba and Devon, I told Vince to contact Paul and let him know we wanted to use them. So Vince did exactly that. A few days later Paul called Vince back notifying him that the Dudleys "had no interest in coming to the WWE."

I looked Vince square in the eye and said, "Is this a rib? You mean to tell me that those two guys would rather play a bingo hall than Madison Square Garden while being paid a tenth of the money?" Seriously? It was bullshit, and I knew it was bullshit. Paul wanted to get WWF talent from ECW, but when it was time to return the favor, the talent wasn't interested?!

The problem was I had no way of proving Paul was lying . . . until I heard from my Deep Throat. There was a guy, a character, a gimmick, who went by the name Blackjack Brown. Blackjack was a wrestling "insider," even before there were wrestling insiders. Blackjack—to this day, I don't know his real name—was a tall, slender, African American guy who always dressed in black and sported crooked teeth and cauliflower ears. How he got cauliflower ears, I have no idea. Regardless, I loved this dude. Blackjack and I stayed in touch for over 30 years, until he recently passed. What a gentleman—the only one who referred to me as "Vicious" because of my "Vicious Vincent" radio days.

So, one day, out of the blue, Blackjack calls me telling me that somebody wanted to speak to me. Guess who . . . the Dudley Boyz.

I got on the phone with Bubba and Devon and not only were they a hundred-percent interested in coming to the WWF but they wanted me to set up a meeting between themselves and Vince . . . which I did. After that meeting, Bubba and Devon were hired by Vince.

Paul had lied—he flat-out lied. And what pissed me off the most was that he was going to deny these guys the opportunity of a lifetime for more fame and exposure—not to mention CASH—in order for him to benefit by having them on his show. I never forgave Paul for that; to me it was a selfish move where he didn't care about Bubba and Devon, and what it could mean to them, their families, and future, but rather he only cared about himself and what their loss would mean to his company. Guess what—then you shouldn't have made the agreement with Vince, and you should have never taken his money.

3. HE'S FULL OF HIMSELF

Ever hear Paul Heyman address a gathering of wrestling marks? My God, he comes across as so full of himself; the arrogance, and pompousness, like he's Jesus, himself, up there giving the Sermon on the Mount. Again, to be fair, I never had a relationship with Paul, so I never really knew the "real" guy. Maybe he is a totally different person outside of the business . . . which I highly doubt, because he has made it clear over the past 45 years—pro wrestling is his be all and end all. Either way, every time I hear Paul speak on wrestling . . . you'd damn near think he discovered the cure for cancer. Again, let me be clear—that is just my take on Paul; millions love the guy.

So, with all that said, this is where you're going to ask, "Vince . . . are you a !@#$%^& IDIOT?"

The answer is *yes*.

There was a point during a conversation with Dixie that Paul Heyman's name came up from a creative perspective. At the time, Paul was on the sidelines and not working for any major wrestling organization. Dixie asked me if I thought Paul could be an asset to the creative, and without hesitation I said yes.

What?

"Vince, with everything you just stated regarding Paul Heyman, you said YES? Are you an imbecile?"

Yes, I AM AN IMBECILE.

But, first and foremost, I am always loyal to the one whose name is on my paycheck. I never stated that Paul wasn't good at what he did—he was—in fact you would have to consider him the genius type. Paul had been around the business forever—he lived it, breathed it, it was part of who he was. He understood the creative process better than the rest, and his ECW run proved that. Some great personalities came out of that company, people we still hold to high regard today—that was because of Paul.

After putting Paul over, Dixie asked me if I would reach out to him, so I did. I had two phone conversations with Paul that went on for hours and hours and hours. Man, I don't know if that was the norm for Paul, if he just liked talking on the phone forever, but during our few phone conversations I could have gotten more words in had I been talking to

Disco (those who know . . . know). Paul just loved to hear himself talk, and in those phone conversations he shared all of his wrestling philosophy and wisdom with me.

The next step was for me to hook Paul up with Dixie, which I also did. I remember a few days later going into her office and asking her if she had spoken to him yet, and how it went.

Dixie shared with me that she had talked to Paul and the conversation went GREAT. "In fact, he's meeting with the Spike executives today at their headquarters in the city," she said.

"Great, what time are you guys meeting with them?" I dumbly asked.

"Oh, no, Vince . . . he's meeting with them alone."

I about fell off my chair. "What?"

"He's meeting with them alone," she repeated.

"Dixie . . . do you know what you just did?" I questioned. "Putting Paul in front of Spike?! He's going to *bury* you, Dixie; he's going to bury the company. His main goal is to sell himself to the network, and he will do that at any cost."

Dixie's face turned pale. As she took in my words, she realized what she had done.

"Oh, he won't do that," she said.

"Dixie, you don't know him—he will. Trust me . . . he will."

Dixie had made a huge mistake, and again it was a lack of understanding the players and the game. So many of these encounters with Bruce, Eric, Hulk, and now Paul were a first for her. She had no idea what she was dealing with. At that point, Dixie got hot at me as she always did every time I tried to smarten her up.

"Are you trying to tell me I'm *stupid*, Vince?" she asked.

"No, Dixie, not at all," I answered. "You just have *no idea* what kind of people you're dealing with."

Paul Heyman was never hired at TNA. Why? I don't know. What Dixie found out, I don't know. If I was right, she wasn't going to tell me anyway, but what came out of the meeting was Spike informing Dixie that TNA needed an executive producer, a person from within the company who could work solely with them involving everything TNA.

Knowing Paul, and doing the math, this was his pitch to the network: "You need an executive producer of that show, and that needs to be me." Forget TNA, he wanted to be working with Spike and that literally would have put him above Dixie and above the company. Well, fortunately that never happened, but what did may have been far worse.

28 CONFRONTING BRUCE

Before I get to that, let me start with this: I never got the chance to talk to Bruce following the meeting where Dixie told me in a very roundabout way that he was now my boss; however, I certainly was going to confront him at TV. So, after the production meeting, I pulled Bruce to the side, and I simply said, "How could you do that to me? Come on, man! I've known you for 20 years. I know how it went down. At the end of the day, I got you a job. I was helping you out. I brought you in here."

This is VERY IMPORTANT, and I want you to take note of it for later on in this book. My voice was cracking, and I was FIGHTING BACK TEARS WITH SOME EVEN SNEAKING OUT.

Yes, I was *so hurt* by what Bruce had done that some *tears actually flowed*.

I'm going to write that again so you'll remember it later: *what Bruce did was so hurtful to me that I cried*.

Bruce of course pleaded his innocence: "Vince, what did you want me to do? She wanted to put me in that spot." Yeah, OK, Bruce, and it was never suggested by you. At that point, I didn't even care. It was all on me. I knew Bruce was going to be Bruce, and I knew exactly what he was going to do when he had the opportunity, so who should I be hot at, me or him? Truthfully . . . neither.

That was all Bruce knew, that was his education in the wrestling bubble. Do whatever you have to do to get the political power that means more stroke and more money. Who you step on doesn't matter—it's just the nature of the beast. Looking back, even though I knew what the end result would be—I did the right thing in trying to get a job for a friend in need.

29 SEND STING HOME

Around that time, I remember yet another incident where Eric managed to pull the pin on the grenade. And it was memorable because it concerned somebody I held in the highest regard . . . Sting.

Steve Borden was by far and away the "realest" person I ever met in my 30-plus years in the business. There was no "Work Steve" and "Personal Steve," there was ONE STEVE, and that guy was respectable, honest, sincere, truthful, kind, and loving all the time. When I first became a Christian, I relied very heavily on Steve, wanting to learn as much as I possibly could about my Lord and Savior. Sting went as far as to pray for me right outside the Fairgrounds in Tennessee, next to an old trailer where some of the wrestlers changed. I will never forget that—you don't forget things like that. So, it's fair to say that Steve was always special to me, and he still is to this very day.

Well, on this particular day, I was at the airport in Denver getting ready to fly out to TV. I get a call on my cell phone from Steve.

"Vince, I'm having a family issue. I can't come to TV."

At the time, Steve was getting a divorce from his wife, and there was a lot of stress going on in his life being that his kids were getting caught up in the unfortunate situation. Now, when you know Sting, you know he is not your typical wrestler. Steve is never going to miss TV unless there is a problem that he absolutely can't resolve. Concerned about Steve and the situation, I'm not even thinking about whether or not he can make the show at this point. "Steve, you do whatever you've got to do. We'll figure it out," I said.

When I got off the phone with Steve, I called Eric to give him the heads up because there were going to have to be some rewrites. Eric's response? "We need to *fire him*. We can't have talent call us at the last minute saying they aren't going to make the show." Eric's response was so quick, I knew there was an agenda there. Without missing a beat, Eric Bischoff went to Dixie and said, "We've got to get rid of Sting."

Thank God, in this case, Dixie felt as strongly about Steve Borden as I did. Dixie knew who Steve was, and she knew that he wouldn't be canceling at the last minute without good reason, but for Eric to jump immediately to "fire him"? Where did that come from? Could he have been a name on Hulk's hit list, with Hulk maybe feeling that Steve's relationship with Dixie was a little "too close" for comfort? Did he not care about the influence that Sting had on Dixie? Who knows. It could be any and all of the above. But to want to get rid of a guy like Sting because he was dealing with a personal issue—that showed me the kind of guy that Eric really was . . . at work anyway.

30 STRUGGLING

At this point, I'm, struggling . . . *really* struggling. Dixie's new structure had made things far worse, as Matt and I were constantly waiting for Eric and Bruce to get back to us so we could finalize the show. To be honest, Bruce wasn't a dick about bouncing it back and was very timely. He wasn't redlining or adding and subtracting elements just for the sake of it. Matt and I never had a problem with his suggestions because Bruce knew I could write, structure, and format a show.

I just wanted to move the process along as quickly as possible—there just weren't enough hours in a day, and we were constantly working against the clock. But now Eric is coming back with all these redlines with no suggestions, just crossing shit out. He's basically attempting to make the statement that I have no idea what I'm doing. Eric took his sweet time in getting the show back to us to the point of it being ridiculous. It was as if Matt and I were his lackeys. It was insulting, degrading, and humiliating, and I just wasn't going to stand for being treated this way—not by him. This was his ultimate revenge on Vince Russo—the guy who exposed him to a point—and he was now going to punish me by working his cunning and conniving magic on a very unsuspecting and naive boss.

STREAM OF CONSCIOUSNESS

Another favorite thing that Eric loves to say about me when he's burying me in an interview is "Vince Russo would throw out an idea and then when you asked him where it was going he'd give you a deer in the headlights look."

He *loves* to say that, actually REVELS IN IT.

What a dick.

In our day-to-day lives, none of us know what's going to happen tomorrow. We all just go with the flow that leads us. That's how I write TV, I've written it that way for almost 30 years. It's called letting things happen ORGANICALLY. If you stay true to your characters and know how all of them would react in any given situation . . . the show writes itself.

Eric always talked about planning and developing "story arcs" for six months, a year in advance—whatever. In my opinion, this was just a dog and pony show, an attempt to show the Spike executives that he was a "TV Guy." But, in reality—do you know how unrealistic that is? On a weekly basis, you are dealing with injuries, suspensions (failed drug tests), disciplinary actions, contract conflicts, elements can affect your talent on any given show in a week, forget in six months to a year. So you spend hours, days, weeks, developing a six-month storyline for Wrestler A, and two weeks in he tears a quad and is out for a year? Do you know how much time you just wasted? And when one wrestler gets hurt, it could have a domino effect on three others.

On top of that, what if your six-month or year-long storyline isn't getting over? You just continue to go with it because it's part of the "arc"? That structure in wrestling is not only unrealistic—it's insane. But, like I said earlier, this was part of Easy's "smoke and mirror show." Throwing around industry buzzwords to make it appear to the network execs that he knew what the !@#$%^& he was talking about.

During the height of the Attitude Era, we wrote from pay-per-view to pay-per-view. Four weeks at a time. We studied the ratings—what worked, and what didn't. We adjusted on the fly, we let the ratings—the audience—decide what they wanted to see. It was a hundred-percent organic.

And, if Eric were listening to his own BULLSHIT, then why did his *83 Weeks* come to an end? Didn't he have award-winning shows in the can for the next 83 weeks?

Guess not.

Guys, one thing about me, and this has been consistent throughout my entire life, if I'm unhappy about something . . . I'm outta there. I'm not going to bitch, moan, and complain to anybody—I'm just going to leave. That kind of attitude came from always having the utmost respect and confidence in myself. If I left TNA, it was going to be their loss and my gain because I would find a new employer who would appreciate me.

Now, I'm sure this is where many of you reading this have been before. At this point, I'm happy to leave, I'm eager to exit, I'm ecstatic about the possibilities for the future, but . . . I also don't have another job lined up. How was I going to support my family? That was always my number-one concern.

When I was in Orlando for TNA, every day I would pray before I left my hotel room, "God, I know you no longer want me here, I know it's time for me to move on, but how am I going to support my family? How?" There were days where I prayed so hard that I CRIED.

I'm going to say that again, but this time I'm going to put it in italics so I can come back to discuss it later: *There were days where I prayed so hard that I CRIED.*

The prayer was so powerful. I just wanted answers from God. I was scared and afraid. I hadn't accumulated millions in my bank account—I wasn't a wrestler . . . just a lowly writer. I prayed, and prayed, and prayed . . . "How am I going to support my family?"

Little did I know, that prayer would be answered in miraculous fashion.

STREAM OF CONSCIOUSNESS

While I'm on the subject of prayer, let me say this: Ever since I've been saved, I've always had a problem with prayer. How can I possibly ask God for anything, with everything he's already given me? How selfish can I possibly be?

It is made clear in the bible, Jesus says that if you are a child of God, "Ask and you shall receive." Can you imagine that? It's just that simple. But I've always had a difficult time taking him up on it. However, in those instances that I did . . . the results were amazing.

31 ERIC BISCHOFF—EXECUTIVE PRODUCER

I swear, as I'm writing this anyone reading is going to think I'm an absolute idiot and they might be right.

So, with the assist to Paul Heyman, after approximately six years on Spike, the network now decides that TNA and *Impact* need an executive producer of the show—more or less a liaison that would serve as the go between for the network and the content creator. In the past, that role had belonged to Jeff, even though he was never officially heralded as the EP.

So here we go again. I raise my hand—"The idiot in the back . . . yeah . . . Russo"—and suggest Eric. No question, Eric had the background with TBS/TNT and knew more than anybody about the television industry. You see how I had no trouble saying that? "More than anybody" includes me. Eric was the best qualified person for the job . . . and he should get it.

But again, let me be clear, Eric working directly with the Spike execs meant an opportunity to soil Vince's good name—and that's exactly what he did. So, Vince, why did you even recommend him? Again—because Dixie Carter was signing my paychecks and it was my responsibility to always do right by the company.

From that day forward, my relationship with the Spike executive on their side, Scott Fishman, turned ice cold. Whereas Scott and I would speak frequently at TV shoots . . . now, we hardly spoke at all. No question Eric was tearing me down to build himself up. But at that point, I didn't give a shit. My mind was made up that I was already gone. It was just a matter of finding the balls to quit without having another job in place. God had yet to answer my prayers . . . so I was waiting patiently.

32 THE JEFF HARDY "INCIDENT"

Before I get into the chapter explaining the one incident that would ultimately end it all for me, I have to talk about the "Jeff Hardy incident" because everybody always wants to know what was behind it. First and foremost, I'm happy to discuss it because it gives me an opportunity to put Easy E over, since I've been extremely critical of him to this point. Whether you believe this or not, I am trying to be fair in the overall picture that I paint of him.

The Universal Studios lot where we housed and filmed *Impact* was huge. I know this because I would log several miles a day, every day, when we filmed there. There were many nooks and crannies in the spacious structure, so it was difficult to account for the whereabouts of all the boys throughout the day. On the particular day of the incident, Jeff Hardy was "rooming" with his friend Shannon Moore in a part of the building that I had never even visited before. But, hold on, before I get any further into that eventful day, I have to rewind about two weeks prior with another incident that is crucial to this story.

It was just like any other TV day, as I was spending the afternoon giving the boys their material for the show. This consisted of going over their matches, pre-tapes, in-ring promos, etc. On this particular day, after

I visited with Jeff Hardy, my Spidey-sense was telling me that Jeff was a bit . . . off. Now, while I had experienced this a few times prior with various talents, you can never be a hundred-percent sure what is causing the "off" feeling. As management, you have to be careful about accusing anybody of anything with the possibility of your allegations being wrong, thus perhaps resulting in a lawsuit.

Add to that, I, myself, have never been under the influence of any substance outside of an Aleve, so, when I was faced with situations like this, I would always defer to one of the boys to make an assessment because the likelihood was that they themselves had once either been personally in this state or at least been around it. On this occasion, I went to D'Lo Brown. I asked D'Lo to go have a conversation with Jeff Hardy because I . . . just wasn't sure.

After spending some time with Jeff, D'Lo came back and said, "Yeah, Vince, he's f***ed up, and no way he can work tonight because he might hurt his opponent or himself."

At that time, Dixie had not yet arrived, but knowing that we were going to have some last-minute changes, I had to call her on her cell to smarten her up about what was going on. Dixie informed me she would be at the building shortly.

Upon her arrival, D'Lo and I explained the situation. Dixie asked where Jeff was, and D'Lo pointed her in his direction. With little time to waste, I started rewriting Jeff's part of the show in an attempt to just make plan B . . . work.

It was about 30 minutes later where Dixie tracked me and D'Lo down. Here's what she said:

"I don't know what's wrong with you guys. Jeff is perfectly fine. He told me that he's just *tired*."

OK . . . I'm tired every day. I'm always tired. This was not tired.

Dixie allowed Jeff to work that night, thank God without incident. So let's fast forward to a few weeks later.

The night of the incident, Jeff Hardy is scheduled to face Sting. Throughout the entire day, there were no warning signs that Jeff might be "tired" like he had been a couple of weeks ago, mainly because nobody had really seen him all day. No doubt he was hiding in one of those nooks and crannies I mentioned a few paragraphs ago.

So the match is set to go on, and Sting makes his entrance from the Gorilla Position. Jeff Hardy's music is cued, and Jeff comes mumbling, stumbling, fumbling, and bumbling through Gorilla as well. No doubt he had planned on showing up at the last second, knowing what state he was in. So, Jeff makes his way to the ring, and Sting knew immediately.

Without missing a beat, Eric Bischoff, who was sitting at Gorilla, hit the ring, and quickly ushered Jeff to the back to prevent any damage Jeff could have caused to either himself, or Sting.

That, ladies and gents, is a PRO. Eric didn't have one second to think, he had to instantly react. With his decades in the business, he had been there many times before and knew exactly what to do in a moment when nobody else did. That is the advantage of having such a seasoned veteran as part of your wrestling company. It's important to understand that. Eric Bischoff was a valuable part to any wrestling company that he ever worked for, but man, it was just that chip on his shoulder that he always seemed to carry around.

But, yeah—thank God Eric was there that day.

33 THE STRAW THAT BROKE THE CAMEL'S BACK

We were one issue away from absolute disaster between myself and Easy E, and it was almost like I was looking for it to happen—no, like I couldn't wait for it to happen. I needed a reason, an excuse, to speed up my departure, and one big blow-up would do the trick.

I had come up with the idea of Bret "The Hitman" Hart becoming the general manager of *Impact*. This was before Bret had ever gone back to the WWE. Oddly enough, "the jack of all wrestling trades" Jeremy Borash had a personal relationship with Bret that I wasn't even aware of at the time. Jeremy told me he would talk to Bret, and if Bret was interested, Jeremy would hook me up with him.

So, Bret was, and Jeremy did.

I got on the phone with Bret, and we had a lengthy conversation. Again, at this point he hadn't yet gone back to the WWE. I wanted to make sure that Bret was interested before I ever brought it up to Eric and Dixie. Once I knew Bret was in, I went to Dixie, who marked out and was a thousand-percent in. Dixie got off on Big Names working for her. She LOVED being Sting's, Kurt Angle's, and Hulk's boss, and now she could add Bret Hart to that list. With Dixie fully on board, I then pitched the idea to Eric.

With no hesitation, Eric let me know he thought it was a solid idea. Whatever issues he and Bret may have had at WCW seemed to be behind him. So, with everybody in agreement, Dixie was at the point of just having to make a money deal with the Hitman.

But, wait a minute . . . did anybody ask Hulk?

The next meeting, where we were supposed to discuss Bret's creative, Eric tells me, Conway, and Ed that Hulk was playing his creative control card. He did not want Bret working at TNA. Supposedly, Bret had said some negative things about Hulk on social media, and therefore—going forward—Hulk would never work with Bret again. Period. End of Story. That's it. Over.

Now, keep in mind, Dixie was the one who gave Hulk creative control, so I'm not going to be hot at Hulk. It was his prerogative to play that card at any time, and in his estimation now was that time. So, that's it. It's over. No Bret.

So now, the three of us meet with Dixie, and Eric has to explain to her the reasons why Hulk wasn't on board with Bret coming in, knowing that Dixie is going to be both disappointed and upset. And Eric begins his diatribe: with the sole intention of protecting Hulk, he begins to tell Dixie all the reasons why we shouldn't use Bret Hart, while never once admitting to her that this was all about Hulk pulling his creative control card simply because he didn't want to work with Bret for personal reasons. Eric starts cutting down Bret—he doesn't look like he used to, he's broken down, Bret could never cut a promo, when I worked with him at WCW he never drew a dime, etc. Now I'm getting upset because I always held Bret in the highest regard. I'm taking objection to this, and I blurt out, "Eric, you're full of shit! Freaking Hulk just doesn't want Bret here. You're not saying that because you don't want Dixie to be pissed at him because she wants Bret here. You're coming up with all these bullshit reasons when you already agreed to it before Hulk's veto. It's bullshit! Just say Hulk's playing his creative card!"

I consider Bret Hart a friend. I worked with Bret Hart for many years. I'm not just going to stand around and allow Eric to talk shit about him when the bottom line is Hulk simply doesn't want to work with him. All Eric had to do was be honest and we would have been fine. That's all he had to do.

This would have been the second time I called Eric out in front of somebody. I did it about 10 years earlier with Brad Siegel when we were at WCW.

To paraphrase the late, great Jim Croce: you don't tug on Superman's cape, you don't spit into the wind, you don't pull the mask off the ol' Lone Ranger, and you never call out Eric Bischoff.

This is the reason that Eric has such disdain for me to this day. I didn't call him out on his bullshit just once, but twice. You just don't do that. I knew his wrath was going to shortly follow.

Man, this was bad—real bad. I knew that there was no way to even attempt to salvage this situation. Things got so bad between Eric and me that Dixie now had to call in her lawyer for a big powwow the day of a TV taping at Universal Studios. I should add that Dixie's lawyer . . . was also Eric's lawyer.

The meeting starts with me simply stating what I had already told Dixie. We all agreed on bringing Bret in, but Hulk used his creative control veto power. Rather than just say that, Eric decided to personally cut Bret down, which I had a problem with.

As the final word exits my mouth, Eric—in magnificent form—redirects the conversation and starts telling Dixie all the things I ever told him about her in our PRIVATE CONVERSATIONS. I had never in my life witnessed anything like this before. I was seeing the mastery of a seasoned politician at its highest level. This was amazing. I had backed Eric into a corner—courtesy of the truth—and in utter desperation he stooped to the lowest of lows.

Eric knew that he now had the ear of a very insecure woman, and Dixie took the chum like a great white that hadn't eaten for days. She literally turned her chair and aimed herself at me. Eric was off the hook. The conversation now becomes Dixie and me and all the things I said to Eric concerning her on a business level. But, here's the good thing—everything I said to Eric, I had also said to Dixie at one time or another. The facts: her not being able to make decisions, feeling more comfortable if others made them for her, etc. There was nothing damaging or earth shattering. So when Dixie asked, "Well, is that true, Vince? Did you say those things?" I said, "Yes, Dixie, I did. but I said those things because they were truthful, and you and I had many discussions about those same points prior."

So now, Eric and I are at the point of no return. Pulling what he pulled . . . to me, he was the lowest form of human being I've ever met in my life. But that's how he played the game, down and dirty like a total snake.

Now let's go back a few pages. Remember I pointed out to you—clearly—two previous instances where I broke down and cried? The powerful praying and the total betrayal of a friend—I had no problem writing that, right? Hell, I'll go even further: I remember crying when a girlfriend broke up with me at 17. Hell, I cry every time Kevin Costner's father comes out of the corn field and asks him if he wants to have a catch in *Field of Dreams*—I actually bawl during that scene. Well, here's the story Eric loves to tell about that meeting, and, logically, knowing where I was with the entire situation at the time, his tall tale is about as ridiculous as it gets.

Eric's claim is that I was exposed as a liar during that meeting, and after being caught . . . I cried. Can you imagine that? Now he's actually never told us what "lie" I was caught telling, much like he's never quite given examples of me being a "pathological liar" over the past 25 years. Was I lying about him covering for Hulk, to avoid Hulk getting heat from Dixie? Is that what I was lying about? And, more specifically—what about the "crying" part? Is there any logic to that at all? What was I crying over? That I was going to be fired from a job I couldn't wait to leave? Hell, that would have been an easy out—I could have collected unemployment.

And you would think if I got caught lying in that meeting that perhaps there would have been some ramifications—like me actually really getting fired. Again, just looking at logic here—if you lie to your boss, and get caught, in any industry in the world—bet the rent you're going to be fired! The truth of the matter was—it was Eric who was lying to Dixie to protect his gravy train, Hulk, and it was me who exposed him as the liar.

You know what this is about? This is the bully on the playground telling all his friends that he made the guy who called him out to the teacher, who exposed him as a liar—cry. "I'm such a big badass that I made him cry real tears"—really? Man, looking back and really diving in, was Eric the kid who was actually teased and bullied as a child himself? Was he made fun of on the playground for, I don't know, maybe his height? Does he now vie to get revenge in his adult life? Perhaps get a black belt, become an arrogant a-hole boss and make everybody's life who worked with him miserable? That's what it seems like.

What a fucking child.

It's over, man. For what he pulled that day, in that room, I would never trust that snake again. There was no fixing this, I wanted nothing to do with Eric and couldn't even stand the sight of him at this point.

But there was still a looming problem: When I quit and give Dixie my notice . . . what am I going to do for money?

34 THE "RETREAT"

In this sequence of events, even though I really can't remember the order in which things happened, I have to tell you about the retreat. Man, this was just more of Eric's absolute bullshit that helped send me over the edge.

Eric comes up with the idea that we need to go on a "creative retreat" in order to come up with story arcs for the next year. Again, as I said earlier, the actors in our play get hurt all the time, causing them to miss weeks and months of work. That is the nature of the job. To spend one minute booking for the next year is such a massive waste of time that we didn't have.

So, of course, Dixie bites, and now I'm heading out on a plane, to I can't even remember where, to listen to Eric's bullshit for three days. Man, I can't even describe to you how !@#$%^& pissed off I was. A creative retreat to book shit six months from now that was never going to happen, when we have a weekly television show to both write and produce *now*. The participants of this bullshit meeting—me, Conway, Eric, Jason Hervey, and some guy sent by Spike who had something to do with SpongeBob.

Now even I'm starting to think I am a pathological liar because this shit can't be true. But . . . it was. Now. let me lay out why Jason and the SpongeBob guy were a part of this.

Jason is there because Eric got his friend a payday—plain and simple. Matter of fact, I never had a single issue with Jason Hervey, he was a hell of a nice guy, which always brought me to wonder, "How could a guy like you have such an asshole as a partner?" And SpongeBob guy? That was another Eric attempt to kiss up to Spike and the Spike execs—by having them both recommend and include a third party into our creative meetings. That would put him deeper in favor with them and guarantee their ear on a daily basis. I never had one single problem with anyone at Spike until Eric was put in that position . . . thanks to me.

Man, I can even remember the car ride from the airport to wherever this place was. My blood pressure was seconds away from exploding my right, left, and center ventricles—all of them.

This is no lie. The entire first day of the meeting, I sat there and said absolutely nothing. Not one word. Every time they went to me, I didn't give them enough words to make a sentence. I was miserable, man; I would have rather been anywhere else. The second day, I had to at least attempt to contribute or else at that point I was the dick.

But this was Eric's MO—all the time—all smoke-and-mirrors bullshit. All show and no go. But—it worked. Spike ate his shit up as quickly as he could serve it on their plate. That's how inept they were.

By the way, I just want to add, that SpongeBob guy? Cool, hipster dude.

35 THE MIRACLE

So it's over. Done-done. I'm at the "get a nanny to watch your kids" point. There is no going back. There is nothing that will keep me at this company shy of Eric either quitting or going home, and neither was going to happen. Notice I said Eric—not Hulk, not Bruce, but Eric. I couldn't work with him. I couldn't work with him a decade earlier at WCW, and I couldn't work with him now.

Every day, before I left my hotel room to go to Universal Studios I would get on my knees: "God, you've made it clear, you don't want me here anymore, I'm not supposed to be here. You have something else for me, and whatever is your will is my way. But, please, how am I going to support my family? What am I going to do for income?"

Again—I prayed so hard and so intense that it drew tears. That's when you know you are really connecting with the Lord.

On one of those particularly miserable days, I remember things were getting so difficult for me that I had to lock myself in the production room, where we held our morning meetings, in the middle of the day just to recenter myself. I took my bible out of my bag and started reading the Book of James. Again . . . I prayed the same prayer for guidance.

As I closed my Bible and opened my eyes, I reached into my pocket for a piece of gum. Weird, isn't it, why was I reaching for a stick of gum at that point. As I take the package out of my pocket, something falls from it—two crisp, neatly folded, right out of the mint, 50-dollar bills. The money was untouched, so new, and so crisp you could almost smell the ink.

I froze. Absolutely—couldn't move. Now, if you know me, you know I never carry money in my pocket—I mean never. Since I started working at 22, I would always pay for everything with my American Express card—still do to this very day.

STREAM OF CONSCIOUSNESS

Here is a helpful hint: only use American Express–it will keep you out of debt your entire life.

I got my first American Express card in 1983. The reason I chose Amex was because when your bill came in you had to pay it in full. There was no monthly installment and no interest accrued–whatever the total was, you paid it. So basically what that meant was that if you knew you weren't going to have the money at the end of the month to settle your bill, then you simply didn't buy what you had your eye on.

I've paid my bill through Amex–on time–monthly–no interest–full amount–for 42 years. And guess what? I've never been in debt in my life.

Hey, Amex–you need to hire me to do a commercial!

Where did this money come from? There had to be a logical explanation. So, I called Amy and asked her if she put any money in my pants pocket, maybe in a pack of gum?

"Why would I do that?" she answered.

So, my wife didn't put it there. Well . . . then, who did?

I remember at that point there was a knock on the door. I slowly got up to open it, almost in a state of trance due to what happened. It was my freelance video/audio guy Dave Bielous.

Let me stop here for a second to say I worked with Dave for years at TNA, just one of the many, many unsung heroes of the wrestling business—Dave worked his ARSE off for me, and I will forever be grateful and thankful. Thank you, Dave.

Back to the money.

Dave looked at me and said, "What happened? You look like you've just seen a ghost."

Well . . . not exactly.

This was God—unequivocally, positively, without a shadow of any doubt. Ever since this bullshit began with Eric, every day it was, "How am I going to support my family? How am I going to support my family? God . . . please show me." I repeated that over and over for weeks, maybe even months. I prayed over it . . . I CRIED over it. Now, "magically," two mint-fresh 50-dollar bills were falling out of my Doublemint.

If I were indeed a pathological liar, this is where I would be caught, being this story is so unfathomable.

But I'm not lying. It happened. And it was a direct sign from God. What he was telling me was, "Vince, I've got you. I know what you need, and I will provide for you. Do what I need you to do."

Now—I had no choice; if I turned back, I would have literally been spitting in the face of God. He was clearly telling me that everything would be OK. As soon as I got home from TV, I called my lawyer, Frank Smith , an absolute godsend in my life. I gave him short, to-the-point instructions: "Frank, do whatever you've got to do . . . get me out of my TNA contract."

36 SAYING GOODBYE TO TNA

There's no question that Dixie was completely blindsided when Frank made that call. I don't think she ever thought that I could be pushed to this point. But . . . I was. This all came about because of her, she allowed it to happen, she was . . . the boss. By not making decisions and allowing herself to be worked by conmen over and over again, never learning from her mistakes, she lost perhaps her most loyal employee over the ten years of her company's existence.

Though our relationship was rocky at times, I was the one who always made an attempt to "smarten" Dixie up. Not that she was dumb by any means, hell, she's far more intelligent than I, but, she had no idea of the game she was in. And it was a game—always was, always will be.

Dixie was way too nice of a human being to ever be a part of that world. That's why I always felt a need to protect her, even if it meant her getting hot at me at times. But now . . . she would no longer have that protection. I was gone.

In the months that followed, it would all come crashing down. Eric, along with his son, Garett, and his company, Bischoff Hervey Entertainment, would up suing Dixie and TNA for "unpaid funds." Hulk played his final creative control card by literally dragging Dixie out of the Impact Zone—by way of his red boot—as she held on for dear life begging him to stay. That really happened. As for Bruce—his relationship with the company ended when Dixie wanted him to move to Tennessee and he declined.

It seemed like only months after I left, all those who were instrumental in my exiting . . . were gone.

SURPISE, SURPRISE!

I have to say this: It's over 13 years ago that I left TNA. You will never hear me say one unkind word about Dixie. Yes, I will tell my story because it is my story to tell, but there is zero ill-will towards her. She was a victim of the wrestling business, as was I.

While Dixie made attempts to try to keep me with the company, I never gave her that chance. There was never even that last conversation. God had spoken loud and clear, and I was now working for him in the capacity of his choosing.

37 GETTING MY OWN SON FIRED

With everything that happened at TNA since the arrival of Eric Bischoff and Hulk Hogan, it's what I'm about to tell you that was the final insult to injury, a reprehensible act of spite that I will never forgive anyone for, not even Dixie.

While Eric and Hulk were employed at TNA, the number of people that they added to the payroll was extensive, and I'm not only talking about the boys, there were paydays for Eric's son, Garett, Hulk's daughter, Brooke, Bubba the Love Sponge, Jason Hervey, Eric's lawyer . . . honestly, I lost track. So when my oldest son, Will, graduated with a degree in film from University of Colorado, and he wanted to get into video production, where better to start than at the wrestling company his dad worked for? Truthfully, I would have never have otherwise put Dixie in the position where she couldn't say no, but after Hulk and Eric got every one of their Huey, Dewey, and Louies in, I said eff it.

Slam dunk, right? No, I had to beg them to hire Will, and the only reason they did was because my last plea was a Vince Russo promo! "Are you kidding me? Eric and Hulk got to bring in Aunt Tilly and Uncle Charlie, but after I worked for you for 10 years—you're not going to hire my son?!"

Will eventually got hired; he even moved out and stationed himself in Nashville. Now, to be clear, Will is not a wrestling fan at all. Matter of fact, he mocks today's wrestling just like his old man does. To Will, wrestling was just a job—just like it was to his old man. So while he was working his ass off, as everybody in TV production does, he didn't particularly love it. I just want to make that clear.

After my lawyer told Dixie I was leaving and nothing was going to keep me there, I heard through the grapevine that my son was going to be fired on my exit. Will was a completely innocent party who did absolutely nothing to deserve such a fate. On hearing this, I told Will he needed to quit to a) not have a "termination" on his resume, and b) to deny them the satisfaction.

Will quit and never came home to Colorado. He moved back to Atlanta to be closer to his girlfriend, Molly, who eventually became his wife and the mother of my two beautiful, angelic granddaughters Amelia and Emery.

STREAM OF CONSCIOUSNESS

Perhaps the most important thing to me in my entire life was for me to be able to keep my family together, in one place. And I did everything in my power to make that happen, but it was just impossible. I guess you can blame me for Will's departure, being that I moved him out of Atlanta in his senior year at high school. While that sounds like I was a terrible father—and maybe I was—you have to understand that I stuck it out in Atlanta for eight years when it was over with WCW in three, because I didn't want to move my family again. But after eight years—I just couldn't take another day there. I'm not a "Southern" type of guy and never will be.

Annie lives in Brooklyn, New York, ironically the city where I was hatched. I was never going to keep Annie in Colorado; she's a free spirit and seems to go where the wind—and her friends—take her. My middle son, VJ, is the only one here. Unfortunately, with his job and responsibilities, I don't see him as much as I'd like.

Being separated from family has really had an adverse effect on me, and I'm writing this because when I'm no longer here, I want my kids to understand how important it was for me to try to keep everybody together. My heart aches because I don't see my kids and my two beautiful grandchildren as much as I'd like.

I will never forgive all those involved for taking my choice of leaving the company and pinning it on my son and making him pay for it. It was low, it was immature, and it was downright bullshit.

38 THE LAST WORD ON ERIC

There isn't anyone I hated working with more with than Eric Bischoff. Not Cornette, not Goldberg, no one even came close. Looking back, even though I'm sure there were some good days, it now feels like every day I was in Eric's presence was miserable. And the sad thing is . . . it didn't have to be that way.

Eric chose to be who he was at work. Yes, it was a decision. He was just never fun to be around, and I never trusted him. If this was his "work persona" as Kimberly Page suggested and I believe, I have to ask: Why? Even coming down to Bernie, who had no idea who Eric was, something changed about TNA the moment he walked in the door.

What's really sad was Eric making it clear that he never wanted to be there—that it was beneath him. TNA was much more than just a company to those of us who helped start it. At its inception, TNA represented hope, opportunity, and family . . . because that's who we were. But then the strangers walked in, all of them merely biding their time while hoping, wishing, and praying that Vince McMahon would call and invite them back to hell.

I constantly get asked, "Did Eric Bischoff and Hulk Hogan Kill TNA?" The answer is . . . in a way. Bottom line is that Dixie couldn't afford to pay Hulk and Eric, and as I stated earlier, it wasn't Eric she was pursuing—he simply came as part of the package. And those two salaries had her robbing Peter to pay Paul: money that should have been spent on PR, advertising, and promotion were going in Hulk's and Eric's pockets. Again—to be clear—that is my viewpoint. But you can't deny the financial situation's bad when Dixie's mother, Janice, is calling me and asking if I could write a show without Sting.

In any case, make no mistake about it, once this book is published, Eric will own up to nothing. These are the words of "Vince Russo, Pathological Liar." Sure. I've sat here and written almost 35,000 words of utter bullshit—I made it all up—it never happened.

Just for the record, I'd like to thank Larry Francis, who emailed various interviews that I was a part of over the years, talking about the very things I stated in this book shortly after they happened. But I really didn't even need his notes; I remember the same things now that I remembered 15 years ago.

This story, this depiction, is how I remember it. Nothing is made up, nothing was concocted by my wild imagination . . . it happened. As I started this book, I promised myself that I wasn't going to go down a road of negativity, but I did, and I know that. The story, the words, they just came out. As I reread the words on these pages, they just scream Eric, Eric, Eric, not Hulk, not Bruce, not Jeff, not Dixie, but Eric. Was it me? Sure, it could have been, but if so, then why weren't there any other problems when it came to my TNA run? Whatever issues I ever had with Jeff, or Dixie, were resolved. They were resolved because when you get down to it . . . they're good-hearted people, Something Eric never was. For me all problems started—and eventually ended—with Eric Bischoff.

But today, no ill will. God lifted all hate from me when I turned over the wheel and asked him to drive. I wish Eric nothing but the best in his future endeavors. But going forward, I'll no longer be the one attempting to "make nice" with him. Over the years, I've wished him a happy birthday and congratulated him on his anniversary through social media channels. I even put over his WWE HOF induction, publicly stating that he deserved it and I was happy for him. I tried for years to take the high road with him, and he never once reciprocated.

39 SO NOW WHAT?

It took a while, but I did exactly what God wanted me to do. He had other plans for me, even though I had no idea what they were. All I knew is that when I left TNA officially in January 2012 . . . I was unemployed and no longer earning an income. I literally had no idea what I was going to do.

As a Christian you fully understand that it's not on your time . . . it's on God's. And God's clock isn't in synch with ours. What could be a year for us could be a day for him. The bible tells you to "be still and listen," and that's exactly what I was doing. In situations like that, you have to align with God as much as humanly possible through both prayer and getting in the word.

But as I waited to get a sign from above . . . I had to do something.

I'd been in this spot before, after I'd left WCW. Once my contract expired, there was no money coming in. Every time I'm put in one of those situations, I usually do one thing: go into business for myself. Prior to ever getting into the wrestling business, I owned two mom-and-pop video stores on Long Island called Will the Thrills Video, after my first son, Will. Once WCW was no longer, I opened a CD Warehouse in Marietta, Georgia. All of those businesses went belly-up, but I far prefer that than having to go work for somebody.

There really isn't anything like being your own boss. Even though the wrestling business didn't make me rich by any means, it did give me enough income to have some options. That's the one thing about having a little nest egg—it can give you choices. I'll never forget what former San Francisco Giants first baseman Aubrey Huff told me. He said, "Vince . . . I have !@#$%^&-you money." Well, I didn't exactly have that much, but I did have enough to open a soft pretzel franchise.

Towards the end of my tenure in TNA, I remember traveling to a house show in Philadelphia. While searching for something to eat, I came across a franchise that I wasn't at all familiar with called Philly Pretzel Factory. Soft pretzels are a way of life on the east coast, especially in Philly. Not being able to pass that gift up, I stopped in and bought a couple of piping hot, fresh, buttery, soft pretzels for cheap.

I was very impressed with the franchise as a whole, so when I started doing some research for my next adventure, I got in touch with the company—this was around July of 2012. After liking what I heard from the franchise director, Amy and I took a trip to Philadelphia together to check it out further. I'm not going to lie; Amy was a hundred-percent against the idea. What did I know about the food industry, for God's sake? But I was getting antsy. I was living off my savings, and no new income was coming in. So, as I've pretty much done my entire life, I ignored my wife's solid and sound advice . . . and I signed the franchise papers.

Interesting side note—I totaled my 1999 Jeep mere minutes after dropping the contract in the mail. Talk about a sign.

Man, a soft pretzel franchise in Colorado . . . Up until that summer of 2012, Philly Pretzel Factory only had stores in the northeast; this was the first time they were going to dip their dough halfway across the country. I knew it wouldn't be the wild success I was saying it would be, and looking back now I can see I was right, but at the time I was doing my best to talk myself into it.

Man, there were problems from the jump. For starters, we couldn't find the right location, even after looking for six months. Finally, we decided on a free-standing booth right outside a movie theater in an outdoor mall. And, when I say booth, I'm not exaggerating—it was tiny. You could barely fit two people inside once all the necessary equipment was set up. And, oh yeah, did I mention, the booth wasn't even big enough to house an air conditioner? That's right, so you have two people, crammed in a booth, with no AC and a very hot oven.

The second issue was that the stores in Philly made their dough from scratch. We weren't able to because there was no !@#$%^& room in the booth to fit the proper equipment needed to do it. So all our product had to be shipped to a distribution center where it was housed and kept refrigerated until I picked it up. The center was about 40 minutes from my house, and I had to make the trip a couple of times a week.

Bro—this was a !@#$%^& disaster from the jump. Add to this—Amy. My wife was miserable; she hated every aspect of this venture. We would argue every night, and she and I NEVER argue. She refused to work in the booth, which forced my hand in hiring kids—and you know how that works.

One of my first hires was a goth girl about 16 years old—she must have been about 5-foot-2 and 90 pounds. Her very first day on the job, she passed out in the booth due to the heat. I literally had to pick her up off the floor and carry her outside. Thank God my middle son, VJ, was around—he seemed like the only one who wanted to help.

Yes—this was as bad as it reads. In the booth, with the oven, the fainting goth girl, and no AC, we also had lye that the pretzels had to first be processed in. If you turned the heat up too high, the chemicals would come boiling over the top, pour all over the floor, and we'd have to evacuate. Then I'd have to walk to the other side of the outdoor mall and go up three flights of stairs to get a mop and a bucket because there was no place in the booth to put cleaning supplies.

Oh, and did I mention we weren't making any money? The outdoor mall was a ghost town. Amy was stressing out real bad. Was this going to be our lives for the next five to 10 years?!

This was a major disaster; a literal and figurative car-wreck in the making.

When I opened the business, I bought a white PT Cruiser that I was going to use for advertising purposes. Because, as I stated earlier, nobody in Colorado had ever heard of Philly Pretzel Factory, I had the company make me two huge logos that I could put on the doors of each side of the car.

The decals that the company made me for both doors were quite similar to what is called a vinyl wraparound (when a company would have their entire vehicle wrapped completely with logos, pictures, art, etc., in an effort to promote their product). Both AEW and the WWE wrap their convoy of ring trucks this way so that when they are out and about on the road, they are a moving billboard, advertising their company everywhere they go. It's a great marketing tool.

STREAM OF CONSCIOUSNESS

Going back to TNA, Bubba Ray Dudley would continuously feed Dixie marketing ideas, just as he had to Paul Heyman in ECW. On this one occasion, I'm sitting in a room with Bubba, Dixie, and Bobby Roode. Bubba is trying to explain to Dixie the idea that I just mentioned—wrapping the ring trucks with TNA promotional material.

"Dixie, did you ever consider wrapping the ring trucks and using them for promotional, advertising, and marketing purposes?" Bubba asked.

"What do you mean?" she replied.

"You know, like the WWE does. Wrap all the trucks with our logo, pictures of talent, like the WWE does."

"What? Like a big sticker?" she said.

Bubba paused. "Yeah . . . you could think of it like a 'big sticker,'" he said.

Dixie answered, "But wouldn't it peel off over time?"

Bubba was growing impatient. "No, Dixie, you can't pull it off, It's permanent."

"Well, what if it's parked somewhere and a teenager or somebody tries to peel it off?" she questioned.

"MOVIN' ON," Bubba said quite loudly as he thought it was best to end the conversation at that juncture.

I drove all around town in that PT Cruiser, just trying to get the word out about my new pretzel company. Even in the freaking fast food industry, I was grinding and hustling my ass off.

STREAM OF CONSCIOUSNESS

THE GRIND.

When I was active in the wrestling business and working my absolute ass off, I would constantly tell myself that it would become easier as I got older. Man, in my 30s, I was flying through it, I was unstoppable, I had so much energy, and I was working off an average of about four to five hours of sleep a night. And those weren't slept-through hours, they were getting up every hour, turning on the TV for ten minutes, shutting it off, turning it on—you get the picture.

In my 40s, I was still going strong; I swear I could've outworked the Energizer Bunny himself. As I was looking 50 in the eye, I slowed down . . . just a hair. I was still going, but I was finding time to rest.

At 60 . . . it hit me like a ton of bricks. This was the milestone where I felt it the most. Six decades in, I knew I had to slow it down. But guess what, boys and girls—the grind never stops.

Being a professional podcaster—which means I get paid good money to do it—has two completely different elements to it with both being vital to your success. For starters, you have to be constantly creating content. There isn't one day where I'm not churning something out. Most of the time I'm doing two to four 30-to-40-minute shows a day. That's on the content end.

Of course, alongside that I need to stay on top of the industry. Watching both WWE *Raw* and *SmackDown* (which I only do because I get paid to, otherwise it would be the very last thing on my dial), staying on top of the business, watching old shows of mine for review and watch-along purposes, etc. Yeah, there's a lot involved—much more than you think—but then comes the hard part . . . using social media to your advantage as much as you possibly can.

I hate social media—I hate it with every fiber in my body. It is a cesspool of living, breathing negativity. The toxicity that one will spew out, nameless and faceless, through their keyboard is playing a large part in dividing this country and infesting it with hate. I would never spend one second on social media if it weren't vital to my business.

Unfortunately, it is.

If I am not on X various times a day, I see a hit in my bottom line. Then you add to that having to balance Twitch and my YouTube channel—that alone is a full-time job. There aren't enough minutes in a day for me to add Instagram, TikTok, or Facebook to my daily routine; it's just nonstop hype and promotion.

If you plan on being a podcaster, just be aware of the social media end of it. Without those channels, you don't stand a chance

Man, the stress was building daily, especially between Amy and me. I had never seen her this upset in the 30-plus years I'd known her. So, one day, I'm driving the PT Cruiser, on the phone with Amy, and she I are in the midst of one of our several daily arguments. I slam my cell phone to the floor of the passenger seat and then immediately bend down to retrieve it. In that split second, my Cruiser struck a road sign right in the middle of a median. The accident took out the entire front end of the car. I remember driving it back home with the entire front end of the vehicle scraping and sparking on the asphalt below. People were staring at me, in disbelief that I was driving the car in that condition. Like a madman, I was laughing at them out my car window, saying, "Nice, huh? You like?" Yeah, man, I had lost my !@#$%^& mind at that point.

This venture was done, and thank God it was over quickly. Much like my businesses earlier, I at least had the foresight to pull the plug before I'd become severely in debt. From the time I sent in my franchise application, July 2012, the entire ordeal lasted 15 months—I was shutting her down in October 2013. Yes, it's fair to say that it was a disaster from the jump. Luckily the owner of the company took some responsibility in failing to properly prepare to extend the boundaries of the franchise, and he actually gave me some of my money back.

I just want to say here on the record, Philly Pretzel Factory is a top-notch company. The product is insanely delicious, and it is run very professionally. But not only was there no taste for pretzels in Broomfield, Colorado, but—even if there was—you would have had to make the dough from scratch, and the product had to be fresh.

Unfortunately, even though this huge mistake and error in judgment didn't ruin me financially, it did indeed set me back. I took a five-figure hit—not to mention the time that was wasted.

OK, God . . . now what?

40 A GLUTTON FOR PUNISHMENT

As I stated at the end of the last chapter, similar to my situation at Will the Thrills Video when Blockbuster came along and I saw the writing on the wall, I was able to put plan B into effect immediately once I permanently closed my Philly Pretzel Factory doors.

I more or less made a carbon copy (you may need to look that up) of that exact scenario in my final Pretzel Boss days, switching to an alternate plan pronto. Even though my praying hadn't stopped, God and I weren't on the same page as far as what my next adventure would be, so I made the mistake of once again forcing God's hand.

Yes—I completely ignored the words of the biblical guidance of "be still and listen."

STREAM OF CONSCIOUSNESS

I made this same mistake over and over again throughout my entire lifetime: not being patient in waiting for God. I know we all have to learn from our own experiences and find it difficult to take advice from others, but I can tell you unequivocally that when you find yourself in the driver's seat, you can bet that you're going in the wrong direction.

I usually like to break it down this way: God created you, which means God holds the blueprint for your life. He clearly created you for a reason—a job, or a task that only you can fulfill. And life is all about him preparing you for that task, making sure that you are ready to take it on and slay it.

But, practically, all of us fall short in the patience department, time and time again. Rather than wait on God, we think we know what's best for us . . . even while we haven't got a single clue. So, we go into business for ourselves, and we fall flat on our face, and we have no reason why.

The reason is simple: it's not about us and what we want, it's about God's will and God's way. I believe you never truly *fail* at anything. Those things that YOU want to do, usually fall short because they're not what GOD wanted you to do, and as I've already stated, if he's not driving the car—be sure that eventually you will crash into that street sign in the middle of a median.

In the waning days of Philly Pretzel, I once again started following the wrestling business online. Where else would I start? It had been my line of work for 22 years at that point. Did I think that God wanted me to go back to that hellhole? Absolutely not. But again, where was the money going to come from? I hated that was even a thought in my feeble mind, having been that God already made it abundantly clear with the two magic 50-dollar bills—"I got this!"

As I followed the latest in TNA, it was incomprehensible to me what was going on at the company at that time. All the players with whom I had any kind of an issue were gone from the company. Jeff Jarrett was no longer active or involved, Bruce Prichard left when he refused to move his family to Nashville, Hogan was gone, and Eric Bischoff went home when he refused to report to Dixie's "New Eric," a former WWE employee by the name of John Gaburick, many calling him just plain, ol' Big.

By that last sentence you can clearly see that one element of Dixie Carter's "business prowess" was still constant—hiring the next guy to make her decisions for her. From Double J to "almost" JR to the tandem of Eric/Hulk, then Brother Love, and now a guy by the name of Big, how many security blankets was she going to go through before she realized that she had a major flaw as a leader that she needed to address?

Anyway, Big worked under Kevin Dunn in TV production at the WWE. I believe he was there when I was, but we never really crossed paths. Seeing this chain of events, I thought I'd reach out to Dixie to see if there may be even the remote possibility of my coming back, now that all my nemeses were gone. Really, man, how ironic was all this? Hulk, Eric, Bruce, all those that Dixie favored over me strictly due to politics, were now gone from the company. Did I find that funny, amusing, and very self-satisfying? Yes, yes, and yes on all counts.

Dixie immediately responded. Why wouldn't she? She never wanted me to leave in the first place, and she had to realize by now that all those bloodsuckers never cared about her interests, or those of her companies. They were all there for personal gain, with every one of them going back to where they came from—Vince and the WWE. And, yes—eventually even John Gaburick would eventually join that club.

Dixie was happy to hear from me, and we had a pleasant email exchange. I don't think we spoke on the phone, but we may have. She told me to get in touch with Big, and we would go from there. Shortly thereafter, I had a few conversations with John. I could tell early on . . . no, let me correct that . . . I could tell almost immediately that it was *Dixie* who wanted me back, with Big not being so welcoming.

This happens all the time in pro wrestling. All the time. It's the reason why the industry just can't get out of its own way. I'm from the school where you hire the best people for the job with the sole intention of making your company better. My entire career, no matter where I worked, I always championed those who would strengthen the company I was working for. Never once did I impede or cockblock anybody out of fear of them trespassing on my territory or eventually replacing me. Reason being—I had the utmost confidence in myself and my ability, and no one was EVER going to outwork me. And if I *was* eventually replaced due to their politics, then it would be the company's loss and my gain. I would just go work for somebody else who appreciated my skill set and work ethic.

I knew immediately that Big saw me as a threat, but he didn't want to undermine Dixie, probably because he really didn't know much about her 10-year history with me. She was also very matter-of-fact in giving him the marching orders to bring me back. I think that Dixie had learned her lesson—that I was right about everybody—and she didn't want me to walk away a second time.

Man, these stories just sound so familiar . . . don't they? This is 2002, where Stephanie and Triple H don't want me back in the WWE because of fear of losing power. There are just so many insecure people in the wrestling business in key spots, and that's what inevitably holds it down.

OK—so here comes the WRESTLING BULLSHIT.

41 THE WRESTLING BULLSHIT

After various conversations with both John and Dixie, they decide that they want to bring me back as a "consultant." What this meant was that I would work from home and never go to the office or attend TVs. Seemed a little strange, but, OK—again—I needed a job. If this was going to get my foot back in the door of a company without Eric, Bruce, and Hulk—great!

But then Dixie said the following: "Vince, no one is to know about this. I don't want anyone to know you are working with us again. And, if anyone does find out—the gig is up."

Those were her exact words and instructions. Dixie never explained why I would be working in such a clandestine manner. Yeah, of course I should have asked her, but I didn't . . . I needed a job.

Let me be clear: I hated this arrangement from the jump. This would fall under the category of wrestling bullshit. This is the nonsense I truly hated about the business. With Dixie wanting to keep everything "top secret," what she was asking me to do was lie. To not be honest. Be deceitful. If you haven't picked it up by now—that's not me, and I had a huge problem with this from the start. And what exactly was her motive?

I firmly believe that Dixie was afraid of the backlash that would be caused by the dirt sheet writers who despised me because I put the entertainment in sports entertainment (aka, wrestling). But, to this day I have no concrete evidence of that. To this day, I have never gotten a reason from Dixie as to why we had to go all eyes-only, clandestine Project Russo. It was a joke; it was bullshit; I did it because I needed a job, but looking back—I should never have agreed to do it.

So, I began my role as a consultant. At the time, the writers at TNA were my young protégé Matt Conway and a former WWE writer named Dave Lagana. Oh yeah, did I mention that I would also find out through a conversation with Sting that Conway was opposed to my coming back to TNA? CONWAY, BRO. This is the guy that I took under my wing at TNA, teaching him everything I knew. I can't even count the number of times that I went to Dean Broadhead, TNA's financial officer, fighting for Matt to get a raise. Man, the hours the two of us spent together writing, creating, formatting, producing . . . we worked on hundreds of shows together—now Matt is going to object to my coming back?!

I will never—never—badmouth Matt Conway. He's one of the most sincere, kind, funny individuals I've ever met. Often, at times, the guy felt like a son to me, but again, me coming back in any capacity now meant the power he had gained in my absence would take a hit—and I understood that. Once Sting smartened me up that I didn't have Matt's vote of confidence, I called Matt on the phone to discuss it with him. I don't remember specifically what Matt's reasoning was, but we did talk it out. Thankfully, we were able to iron everything out, and I was eventually, secretly, brought back into the fold.

So I begin my top secret consulting role with TNA. I would have phone conversations with Matt and Dave, and that would be the extent of it. It was my first time ever working with Dave Lagana . . . and I wasn't too impressed. His gimmick was that he would never throw out an original idea of his own, he would just piggyback on the creative of others. That's how you stay "safe" in your job. That way a bad idea is never yours; if it shits the bed, it's somebody else's fault.

It felt like it was only a couple of weeks before I was already writing the entire show, even though my role was to just give my thoughts, ideas, and feedback. But I didn't mind, I was working to getting back full-time anyway.

Unfortunately, what I did find out in a hurry was that it was going to be extremely difficult for this to work without me being "hands on" at TV.

This became evident when I would write numerous pre-tapes into the show, only to find out, when the team came back to Nashville, that the pre-tapes were never shot in Orlando. This would have never happened had I been present at those shows. Pre-tapes should always be a priority, and you must get them all shot no matter how much, or how little, time you have. If it means starting early or finishing late, you get them done.

So, when you don't have the pre-tapes shot, what does that mean? Simple—more lame-ass, mean-nothing, fake wrestling matches on the show. That's how you become a rasslin' show just like all the other rasslin' shows. Their lack of effort was really disappointing to me, but in the spot I was in there was nothing I could do . . . or say.

My role as a consultant soon went to the next level. A few months in, and I now flew to Nashville to meet with Dave, Matt, and Big in person. I was less impressed with Lagana in person, but trust me—that was the least of my concerns. Within the first 15 minutes of sitting down with Big, I could tell that he thought he knew more about creating, writing, character development, and storytelling than I ever did. Maybe he was flexing his muscles . . . who knows, and who cares, all I remember was saying to myself, what the hell do you need me here for if you !@#$%^& know everything. I could almost see immediately why he and Eric wouldn't have worked out. You can't have two egomaniacs at the head of the table. But again, I needed the work at the time, so I ain't saying shit.

During this period, I keep asking Big when I was going to be able to come to TV. Letting him know I'm never going to be able to contribute the input I need to unless I'm there. Big kept telling me to be patient, which I was because I had no other choice. Then finally, after coming back from TV, Big told me he spoke to Scott Fishman (the Spike exec I told you about earlier). Big said, "I told him you were consulting for us—he didn't have an issue with it." That was great news. I had no idea what damage that Eric had done in my relationship with Scott, but with Eric no longer there—everything seemed to be cool. Big said that now, since Scott knew, it was only a matter of time before I would be invited to TVs.

42 NO WAY ALL THE EGGS ARE GOING IN THE TNA BASKET

Please heed this advice . . . If you are hungry, self-made, and a go-getter, you want to listen closely to me here:

NEVER PUT YOUR EGGS IN ONE BASKET.

Don't. Ever. Too many things can happen that are just out of your control. You could be employee of the month on Monday and shit-canned on Tuesday—it can happen that fast. Always have a plan B, and, if you're smart, also a plan C and a D.

While I was indeed trying to get my foot back in the TNA door, I certainly wasn't banking on it. I was exploring other avenues in which I could make a living, and that's when I came across a certain individual I'll call Mr. X. Mr. X was to introduce me to and school me in the latest trends in technology that I could benefit from by utilizing my knowledge and background in professional wrestling. The main outlet was podcasting, something I knew zilch about at the time.

Now, I'm not going to put a name to Mr. X because he screwed me over in the end by attempting to hold me up for money. Prior to starting our relationship, we both agreed to the terms between us, only for Mr. X to attempt to change them a short time in. Sorry, man, I don't go for that bullshit. We made a fair agreement that we were both happy with, and I expect you to honor that. Since you didn't—I'm not going to honor you by putting your name in my book.

Despite the ugly falling-out that we had, I was, and still am, extremely thankful to Mr. X for introducing me to the world of podcasting, YouTube, Twitch, Twitter (now X), Facebook, and all the other social media tools I would need to know and understand in order to go into business for *myself*, and not have to depend on people like Big to feed my family and support my vinyl addiction.

STREAM OF CONSCIOUSNESS

As of this moment, I have 4,344 albums in my vinyl collection. My wife calls me a hoarder—I like to label myself a collector. In the basement of my home, I have what I call the music room, where I house all my records and music paraphernalia. It is my pride and joy, my safe haven, my sanctuary, whatever you want to call it.

I have albums in every category—pop, metal, easy listening, Italian music, folk, country, children's, singing celebs, soundtracks, jazz, blues, R&B, death metal, classical, and perhaps the greatest assortment of Tiny Tim records you will ever find anywhere.

Here are the 25 MUST-HAVE ALBUMS that should be in every collector's sanctuary:

The Beatles—*Rubber Soul*
Meat Loaf—*Bat Out of Hell*
Anita Baker—*Rapture*
Bachman-Turner Overdrive—*Bachman-Turner Overdrive II*
Paul McCartney and Wings—*Wings over America*
Tenacious D—*Tenacious D*
Journey—*Escape*
Rihanna—*Rated R*
Elton John—*Goodbye Yellow Brick Road*
AC/DC—*Stiff Upper Lip*
Liza Minnelli—*Live from Radio City Music Hall*
The Beach Boys—*Good Vibrations—Best of the Beach Boys*
Elvis Costello—*Armed Forces*

Talking Heads—*Stop Making Sense*

Carole King—*Tapestry*

KISS—*Lick It Up*

John Mellencamp—*The Best That I Could Do 1978-1988*

Jim Croce—*Photographs & Memories: His Greatest Hits*

Tom Jones—*Tom Jones Live in Las Vegas*

Simon & Garfunkel—*The Concert in Central Park*

Billy Joel—*The Stranger*

Boston—*Boston*

Vision Quest (Original Motion Picture Soundtrack)

Bleachers—*Strange Desire*

Alvin and the Chipmunks—*Christmas with the Chipmunks Vol. 1*

I love music, man, it is my absolute getaway. For years I have been a Thrift Store Addict, where I just bounce from store to store looking for "treasures" that are not already in my sanctuary. Over the years, it has gotten more and more difficult to actually find something that I don't own—unless it's a new release.

Amy is always making me "Lower the music!" (a request she makes by screaming over it), whether I'm in my safe haven or my 2000 Jeep. My wife continuously reminds me that I'm not going to be able to take my precious vinyl with me when I'm dead . . . and that's the point—I want to leave them behind for my kids and grandkids. My album collection will tell them who I was. Not any old wrestling video that they can find on YouTube—that is the furthest thing from me that you could imagine. I've already given them instructions: "If you part with just one of my Liza albums, I will come back and haunt you for the rest of your lives."

So, as I was working my way back inside TNA, I was also building my online presence, Pyro and Ballyhoo, which would later become RussosBrand—the same moniker it holds today. RussosBrand has been going strong for about a decade now, and it's how I've made my living for about that long. But, again, I thank God for giving me the foresight to fully know and understand that laboring inside the wrestling business wasn't going to work, no matter how badly I needed to earn a paycheck. It was never God's plan for me; he simply used it to get me from point A to point B, which I will explain a little later.

43 EASY E STRIKES AGAIN

If I had read what I am about to tell you in a dirt sheet, I would have absolutely, positively, unequivocally, without a shadow of a doubt thought that it was bullshit, no question. But I didn't read this in a dirt sheet . . . I experienced it.

So, according to Eric himself, he went and sat home when Dixie told him he would be reporting to "Big" John Gaburick. And, I can't say that I blame him. You just can't change the rules of a contract. I went home from WCW after three months for the same reason. They wanted to go from my contract stating I was the "Head of Creative" to me being part of a "Committee." I said "thanks, but no thanks," and I went home, and WCW had to pay me.

That's the same reason why TNA was going to have to pay Eric Bischoff. Now, I can't state that the reason the following took place is a hundred-percent correct, but logically it makes all the sense in the world.

So, Eric goes home because he doesn't legally have to abide with TNA's "new" structure based on his "old" contract. But hell, if he's going to be sitting at home and we're going to have to pay him, we're going to put Eric to work. Let's see . . . what can we have him do . . . ? Hmmm . . .

I GOT IT!

How about we ask Eric to critique all the episodes of *Impact*, which he is now *not* a part of?

Great idea, right? Wrong. Not when Eric is CCing his weekly reviews to the brass at Spike as well. Are you !@#$%^& kidding me? This is hundred-percent fact because Eric's emails after every *Impact* were being forwarded to me. So, I saw the original email that Eric sent out where he was sending all his comments to Dixie, Big, and the head honchos at Spike. He wasn't even trying to hide it by BCCing them. He was sending the message to Dixie and Big that he was also emailing to anyone who matters at Spike!

Eric would trash every show in this weekly report, burying everybody and everything. He didn't have one positive note at all. So what Eric—who was at one time the executive producer of the show—was really saying is that the two people currently running TNA—Dixie and Big—don't have a !@#$%^& clue what they are doing.

And, remember, the execs at Spike loved Eric. He bamboozled them into thinking he was all that from that very first "Hulk Hogan Dog and Pony Show." So what could Spike have actually thought about Dixie sending Eric home when he refused to report to Big? One can only imagine the picture of Big that Eric painted to Spike. I'm sure—no, I'm hundred-percent positive—it was very similar to the one he painted of me to those same people! But to have the absolute nerve and gall of not even trying to hide it—that is the arrogance of Eric Bischoff in a nutshell.

Please remember this vital chapter when we visit the question of who was responsible for ending the TNA–Spike relationship in the pages to come.

44 I F***ED UP

Over the weeks, my consultant role began to grow a bit more. The next step was me working with the TNA announcers Mike Tenay and Taz. While at TNA, I had an extremely close relationship with both these guys. One of the highlights of my week was going over the shows with them a couple of hours before we aired. Man, during those sessions, Taz's humor would just floor me. The dude has one of the driest senses of humor of anyone I've ever met. That's why he's still going strong at AEW today. Taz and I still have a great relationship currently, and we text each other lines from *The Honeymooners* on at least a weekly basis. After his TNA stint, Mike chose to walk away from the business and retire—smart man. But could today's wrestling business use Mike Tenay, or what?!

So, it's clear to see that my foot was getting close to actually being in the door; the only thing left was my showing up at TV.

Unfortunately, this is where things went south in a hurry. And I didn't just stub my toe in the door; I broke my entire ankle, foot, and all five toes.

One day I was sending a business email to Mike and Taz. As I typed in the name Mike, because I hadn't emailed him in a while and I forgot his address, I accidently sent the email to another Mike—whose surname I won't give here because I wouldn't even be able to stomach reading it in my book—who happened to be a dirt sheet writer. Now, keep in mind that there was much speculation that I was somehow linked to TNA at the time, but no one was really sure. This was the evidence they needed.

Without hesitation, this Mike ran with it. Never contacting me first—like any Real Journalist would—and saying, "All right, Vince, the gig is up, are you going to break the news . . . or am I?" Man, just yet another reason why I loathe those dirt sheet hacks. Unfortunately for me, since this was Dixie's little secret, word getting out could cost me my job, just as she had warned. When I realized what I had done, I had to call Big to let him know. He was livid that the word got out—LIVID!

Seriously, though, are you !@#$%^& kidding me? You want to play this childish game of "Vinnie's got a secret" and then get hot at me because it gets out, like somehow, someway, it wasn't bound to anyway? I remember Taz not talking to me for over a year because he was convinced that I "purposely" let the cat out of the bag. I wonder who convinced him of that? I got in an argument with Taz, just asking one simple question . . . Why the f*** would I do that?!

This was a big deal, and perhaps the out Big needed to keep Vince Russo from ever getting back with TNA full-time.

But this would be just the tip of the iceberg.

45 HOW DOUBLE J FOUND OUT

Before I get to Armageddon, let me tell you about another situation that this ridiculous "little secret" sparked.

Man, Dixie put me in a really tough spot when she made it clear that "if anybody finds out about this . . . it's over." The first person that came to my mind was Jeff Jarrett. Jeff had found his way back into TNA . . . again . . . but it was clear that both he and Dixie were taking it slow. I guess Easy E refusing to report to Big may have opened the door back up for Double J. Man, you are asking me to keep this from a friend, a former brother, the reason why I ever saddled up with TNA in the first place. This was wrong on so many levels.

Again, I didn't have a choice; I needed a job and the money. If that same situation arose today, I would just say no—I'm not going to do that. But today, I'm in a much different position—a hundred-percent attributed to finally listening to God.

One day, Jeff is sitting in Dixie's office when the two of them bring Janice—Dixie's mom—in on a call. Janice doesn't know Jeff is in the office. Before Dixie can say anything, Janice asks, "So, how are things working out with Vince?"

That's how Jeff found out. Jeff cut me off; he completely stopped talking to me from that point on. I'm not really sure what he wanted me to do when Dixie gave me the "rules" that went along with my consulting opportunity. Matter of fact . . . I'm sure that he would have done the same thing if he were in my shoes.

But, I'm not going to deny, that was a shitty way for Jeff to find out. And if it were up to me, everybody would have been told up front . . . but it wasn't up to me.

Years later, I would see Jeff and Karen at a convention where Karen pulled me aside and told me that Jeff didn't stop speaking to me because he found out about the consulting. He stopped speaking to me because Dixie told him that I spoke negatively to her concerning him.

Really? And after over 20 years of friendship Jeff isn't going to call me and ask me if it's true? But again—that's wrestling, and that's how it works. Thankfully, Jeff and I were able to reconnect over the years, and I'm very grateful for that.

But during that time it was all wrong. It was all so wrong. I remember Dixie had me on the phone with Jeff and the creative team, with nobody but her knowing I was listening to every word . . . That was such bullshit: wrong on every level. But, again, I have to take full responsibility. I could have said no . . . but I didn't.

46 THE SHIT HITS THE FAN

All this happened at once, and it now feels like it was supposed to be happening at once. It was as if God was saying, "If you're not going to get out of this godforsaken business yourself, then I'll gladly do the honors."

Once the gig was up and Dixie's little secret was out of the bag, I got a call from good ol' JR, asking me to be a guest on his podcast. At that time, JR had established himself in the young podcasting business, and being a guest on his show would have been a great boost for my platform.

Given the touchy circumstances at the time, I told JR that I had to call Dixie first to make sure it was cool. Keep in mind, I was doing that as a courtesy. I was consulting for TNA, I wasn't a contract employee. They had no authority to tell me what I could and couldn't do when it came to growing my own brand.

I emailed Dixie when I got off the phone with JR and told her about the opportunity. Dixie was on the fence about it, repeating a few times, "Vince, I don't want you talking about your working relationship with TNA." I told Dixie I wouldn't, and then I stated that I would call JR right back to make sure it was cool with him.

So, I immediately called JR and told him about Dixie's concerns, and he assured me that there would be no TNA talk whatsoever. If you know JR, you know he's a man of his word. I had zero reason to believe that he would go down that road with me when I asked him not to.

I then emailed Dixie back and told her about my conversation with JR, and him being a hundred-percent cool about not discussing TNA. After that email, I never heard back from Dixie. I took that as a sign of her saying it was OK, as long as JR committed to not mention my role in her company.

The next day, I did the interview with JR . . . well, not really an interview, more like a discussion. And JR never once brought up TNA—just as he had promised. Later that day, I get a call from Big, and he was livid—once again—that I did the interview with JR. I told Big about my email exchange with Dixie, letting him know that I never heard back after informing her that JR made it clear that he wouldn't bring up TNA—which again—he never did.

So, what was Big's issue anyway? TNA was never !@#$%^& discussed. From there Big said that Dixie sent me a follow-up email, after my last message to her, stating that regardless of what JR said, she didn't want me to do the interview. And even though she told me not to, I did it anyway.

To this day, I don't know if Big was full of shit, or not. All I know is I never received that follow-up email he was talking about. When I relayed that to Big, he said perhaps the worst thing anyone can say to me. He said, "Vince, you're a liar."

Again, guys, think about the logic here. If there was a follow-up email from Dixie stating that I was not allowed to do the interview with JR, that would have caused a problem—a huge problem. I can tell you this, I certainly wouldn't have said, "Oh, OK, Dixie, whatever you say—as a consultant, you own my ass!" That would have never happened. There would have been a lengthy conversation between Dixie and me—no doubt.

Big referred to me as a liar a few times, and I could feel the Italian temper start to boil. I told Big that I would send my hard drive to Nashville and pay for the shipping myself so they could go through all my emails and see that the one he was talking about didn't even !@#$%^& exist.

Then Big absolutely exploded me. While laughing at me, thinking this was all funny, Big said, "Vince . . . now I understand why nobody likes you and nobody can get along with you. Now I know, everything I've ever heard about you is a hundred-percent true."

I lost it. I went full-blown J.J. Dillon promo circa 2000 on him. I cussed him up and down, using every profanity-laced word I had ever heard in my life. This was Big's out to get rid of me once and for all. God only knows what he went back and told Dixie about our conversation. I'm sure he left out the parts about the email that didn't and never did exist and his provoking me by calling me a liar numerous times over.

BREAKING NEWS!!!

I was just able to find the ORIGINAL EMAIL I sent Dixie on July 31, 2014. Here, copied verbatim, is the proof that everything I said was a hundred-percent true. (Obviously I can't post Dixie's email address.)

> From: vincerusso@xxxxx.com
> To: dcarter@xxxxx.com
> Sent: Thu, Jul 31, 2014, 5:27 p.m.
>
> Even though it is a non-issue now, I just called my IT guy for pyroandballyhoo.com, and he reminded me that there's a free download called TEAM VIEWER that he uses to log onto my computer. Once he's in—he has access to everything I do.
>
> I just want to offer you the opportunity to get that free download, and log onto my computer, so that you can see with your own eyes, what I did, and did not receive from you on Monday. If it's not in my old mail—my only option was to have deleted it. With Team Viewer, you can go through all my deleted mail as well.
>
> My integrity was questioned not once, not twice, but three times over the last two weeks. I think you at least owe me this opportunity to indeed show you and John that I never received your second email.
>
> This has nothing to do with me wanting my job back, but everything to do with me showing you and John that I am a man of my word.
>
> If you chose not to do this—I understand—but, I no longer think you have the right to question me if you don't want to look the proof in the eye.

> Yeah—this is all meaningless BS to the both of you now, as you and John—have much bigger fish to fry—but, I don't want to go out being labeled "dishonest" without having the opportunity to prove otherwise.

And there you have it.

At that point, f*** Dixie, f*** Big, f*** TNA, and f*** wrestling. It was over. F*** these people and the donkeys they rode in on. I was going into the Vince Russo Business, balls to the wall. No longer was I ever again going to put my future or my fate in anybody else's hands but mine.

As the GREAT Bin Hamin would say, "F*** 'em!!!"

47 SWEET, SWEET KARMA

Karma is my favorite word. I love the sound of it and what it represents. The meaning to me is simply this: if you're a dick and you do the wrong thing, you are going to get yours!

And make no mistake about it—it may be a day, week, month, year, decade, but karma will catch up with you and get you!

I can't tell you how many people in the wrestling business were eventually dropped on their heads by karma, after treating others shitty or just doing shitty things in general. Best-case scenario may be the big kahuna himself, Vincent Kennedy McMahon, and trust me I'll have an entire chapter about that later.

I can remember John Gaburick bringing me to his house in Nashville. He bought the property when he was hired by Dixie. Maybe twice the size or more of any house I had ever lived in. It was in a gated community and yeah . . . rich people lived there. Big was living high on the hog when Dixie hired him, God knows what his salary was; I'm sure at least three times what mine was when I worked for the company.

When I was employed all those years at TNA, I made roughly about $100,000 a year. I know I was worth well more than that, but I also knew that this wasn't the WWE. TNA was always on a budget, always, and I just wanted to do my part to help. Man, God only knows what guys like Eric, Hulk, and now Big were getting paid. Honestly, I don't want to know because if I did, I'm confident I would vomit.

The first house I ever lived in when I moved to Trumbull, Connecticut, to work for the WWE would literally fall under the category of one of those "tiny houses" that we see today. I had three kids in that house. It was so small that after buying the sectional of my dreams—for well under a grand—I realized that it was too big to fit in our family room, so for years part of the couch was in the hallway.

But Biggity Big . . . he was living in a castle. I asked myself, "Why would anyone buy a house this big even if they could afford it?" Yeah, man, getting that spot at TNA made John's head so big it almost hit those vaulted ceilings that only certain people can afford. But that's cool. Some may say he even deserved it, and maybe he did, but, brother—that day on the phone to me, him laughing, etc.—yeah, it was just a matter of time before karma ate him up and spit out whatever was left.

But again, man, it's not the "playa" as Booker T would say; it's the *game*. And there's no doubt in my mind that John Gaburick was a good man, husband, father, son, friend . . . but, like Easy E, you can throw all that out of the window when the wrestling business sticks its claws in you.

Yeah, karma came in a big way, a huge way. It came in the form of Spike not renewing its contract with TNA Wrestling so they were gone, gone, gone off the channel they had served for nine years. To think that TNA once drew over two million people on Spike is amazing. Yes, that was under my pencil, even though my critics will tell you what a "failure" I was at that company. Failure? You know what AEW would do today for those numbers? They can't even muster half of that on a network twice the size.

The story goes that Spike offered a new contract to TNA, Dixie held out for more money, Spike then pulled the deal off the table, and it was "Goodnight, Irene." Now, I can't confirm that, but that's what I was told.

Unless . . . you want to believe the story that "Hillbilly Jim" Cornette tried to spin.

48 HILLYBILLY JIM'S TNA/SPIKE STORY

I never talk much about Jim Cornette. I'll only answer questions if they're brought up in an interview. When you know Jim and understand Jim, you learn quickly to not engage Jim. And there is good reason for that. For as brilliant a mind as JC has for the wrestling business, he is also childlike and has never grown up.

This becomes evident when he doesn't like somebody—take me, for example. Jim immediately goes to fourth-grade recess, when you're allowed outside for 30 minutes after you eat. During that time, one 10-year-old is usually in a war of words with another 10-year-old. That's usually where you'll hear the phrase "shit stain." Jim Cornette, almost in his mid-60s still refers to me as a shit stain. Do you think I'm actually going to engage with anybody who's still just starting puberty at 64? Responding to this would be the equivalent of fighting with a child, whose sole offensive tactic is name-calling. He may even use this as a finish when he runs out of kindergarten expletives: "And, and I'm gonna PISS ON YOUR GRAVE when you die!"

Yes, Jim plans to "piss on my grave" when I die. Hate to break the news, James E., but I've instructed my family to cremate me upon my extinction. So guess you'll be pissing in my urn. You're going to have to alter your act now.

And that is why this story is so comical.

So, Spike decides not to renew their contract with TNA. It happens all the time in business. Sometimes deals just go awry.

But, for dirt sheet writers in wrestling, there always has to be an *angle*, something *sensational*. Dirt sheet hacks thrive off of controversy and drama—they eat it up. So, in this case, Dave Meltzer was told by a "source" that the reason Spike didn't renew their deal with TNA was because they found out that Vince Russo was consulting for the company.

I have to pause for a second because that line is so !@#$%^& ridiculous.

Think about that and then try to apply any logic whatsoever to it. Now, as I stated earlier, Big told me that he informed Scott Fishman, a Spike exec, that I was consulting for the company. John said that Fish was cool with that. OK, for argument's sake, let's say Big was lying. Let's say he never even told Fish. Let's go one step further, let's say Big indeed told Scott, and Fish was livid!

Process that for a moment.

Now, if such were the case that Spike didn't want me consulting with TNA—hypothetically—then wouldn't it be common sense for them to tell Dixie that? Simple, right? "Dixie, we don't support Vince working for TNA as a consultant. It would be in your best interest to terminate that agreement." So, Dixie terminates the agreement with me and all is copacetic with Spike. Reasonable—makes sense, right?

Not in Meltzer's world. On whatever planet he lives on, a cable network, Spike, is going to ixnay renewing a nine-year relationship they have with the highest-rated show on their network, *TNA Impact*, because they don't like a consultant that the content provider is using? We are talking about a multi-million-dollar contract here, and it is going to fall to pieces because Vince Russo is giving you advice? Wouldn't it have just made sense—if any of this is even true, which it's not—for Spike to say . . . "just stop using him"?

This is why guys like Dave and all the other dirt sheet hacks get zero respect from me. Everything is about grabbing a headline and being the first to report. Also, keep in mind that at the time the TNA/Spike negotiations fell apart—I was already gone from the company. I had nothing to do with TNA at that point.

So, when grilled about his "source" after his ridiculous report was blown to hell, Dave let slip that it was Cornette who told him. Now, keep in mind—Cornette hadn't been working for TNA for years when this all went down.

This is how you smear the Vince Russo name. Cornette made the shit up, and Dave reported the shit as factual. Meanwhile, did Dave even consider asking Dixie Carter herself? Of course he didn't. Just listen to the guy who has a 25-year-old beef with the guy he's blaming this all on. What a !@#$%^& joke.

But that's not the only time that I caught Dave with his hand in the "Vince Russo bullshit" jar.

49 MELTZER

Dave Meltzer has made himself well over a million dollars working from the "outskirts" of the wrestling business. Make no mistake about it—he has never been *in it*. He has never worked for a major wrestling promotion, nor has he ever been welcomed inside the locker room of industry leader WWE. All the news Dave reports is generally not firsthand, it mainly comes from his "sources," who of course he never names. But you have to give credit—he's benefitted greatly as an outsider. Al Snow calls Meltzer the "greatest worker in the business" . . . and he's right. So, yeah, man, I will give the guy his due. By labeling himself an "expert in the field," he has pulled the wool over many a person's eyes for decades, while taking money from their pockets at the same time.

The issues I have with Dave are various. For starters, when he's wrong about a report, I've never seen him retract anything. I was a victim of this when I went out to *Lucha Underground* to get some content for Pyro and Ballyhoo, and Dave reported that I was meeting with the company brass in an attempt to get a job. The names he was listing—I never even heard of these people . . . had no idea who they even were.

So I emailed Dave to inform him that he was a hundred-percent wrong on his story. I asked him to retract it, and of course he never did. Again, man, if you're going to make the claim of being a journalist, then you should act like one. When you give out false information, it is your duty and responsibility to own up to it . . . Dave never does.

Another pet peeve of mine is that Dave will just "throw shit out there," never backing it up with proof, facts, or numbers. He loves to tell anybody that will listen that the ratings went down in my first three months at WCW when, in fact—they went up. The numbers are there for anyone to see: WCW ratings before Russo; Russo's first three months; after Russo left. Those numbers paint a very clear picture of the influence I had during my time there.

I even went as far as to post those ratings publicly, numerous times . . . do you think for a minute that I would claim that the ratings went up if they didn't, knowing that anyone could do the research and find those numbers? I'd have to be some kind of an absolute moron. But that's exactly what Dave has done, and he's done it over and over again.

Maybe I take exception to this more than others, but that's mainly because I have a degree in journalism, and I have actually put some time in at radio and TV stations and a daily newspaper. I take great, great pride in what a *true* journalist represents. I, myself, on several occasions have had no problem in saying that I was wrong or that I made a mistake. Nobody is ever going to get it right all of the time; but apparently, Dave Meltzer does—he must be an exception to the rule. He is always correct, even when proven wrong by facts, numbers, evidence, and actual proof.

I'll have more on Meltzer a bit later when I discuss today's wrestling business—a business that, unfortunately, Dave now has great influence over.

50 RUNNING OUT OF OPTIONS

While still waiting to hear from God, my options as far as employment goes were dwindling. After the failed pretzel booth and the explosion with Big, there just weren't many opportunities. I was now in a very familiar position, one I had experienced many times prior throughout my life . . . I had to roll the dice and gamble on myself.

Thank God I had the foresight to start Pyro and Ballyhoo as a side hustle. Without planning on it, this became my main job and source of income far sooner than I expected. Again, to give the credit where it belongs, Mr. X gave me an education on how social media worked. Up until that point, I had no knowledge or experience of it because I just didn't need it. Now I was fully depending on it. I started pyroandballyhoo.com, where I wrote numerous blogs every day. Mr. X even showed me how to upload pictures to all my stories. Man, I was taking such great pride in the site: it was mine, and I was doing it my way with no one else dictating their bullshit to me. I was so driven; this opportunity was maybe what God had in store all along.

The site was really starting to grow some steam, but of course, as is the case when you are attempting to make a living on social media—the money wasn't coming in. I was cool with that because I didn't expect it to happen overnight, I knew it was going to take time. Unfortunately, I think Mr. X felt a bit differently. I think he believed that the money would come in much quicker. So, not meeting his expectations, Mr. X contacted me when I was shopping in Target with my wife.

Prior to going into business with each other, Mr. X and I entered a verbal contract. There were no lawyers or signatures involved, just simply a handshake. I had no issue with that because up until that point I had no reason not to trust Mr. X. That changed with a series of text message. Mr. X wanted to change our agreement so he would be compensated more . . . and me, less. He threatened to shut down the entire site if I didn't agree with his demands.

I cannot tell you how many times I have had this same issue with wrestling marks over the years who say they're going to help you, only to wind up screwing you. I don't know if there is a sense of power in !@#$%^& somebody over in the business as revenge for never making it in. Whatever the reason, it has happened to me ad nauseam.

My answer to Mr. X was simple—we had an agreement, and I expected him to live up to it. I had no intention whatsoever of changing anything. I wasn't going to be victim to his threats, so go ahead and shut the site down.

In the position I was in, I had zero power. I didn't know anything from a technical aspect. I hundred-percent trusted that he was working in my best interest. I knew he had full access to the site, I knew he could shut it down, but he sure as hell wasn't going to hold me hostage over something with my name on it. So, go ahead—shut her down.

I don't think that was the response that Mr. X had anticipated because now, without me, he had nothing. So basically, he had wasted all that time and effort to walk away with nothing. At that point, I had to get my lawyer, Frank Smith, involved again. Mr. X informed Frank that he was looking for a settlement for me to take over the site. I said, "No !@#$%^& way." I wasn't giving that dude a dime. I'd rather start again from scratch.

Knowing it was in my best interest to build upon what I had already started eight months earlier, rather than start anew, Frank paid the settlement without my knowledge, which I found out after the fact. It wasn't a lot of money, but it was just the principle. Mr. X, the mark that he was, of course would go on the Internet and attempt to smear my name. Good for him. Here I am over 10 years later still going strong and nobody has heard from him since.

STREAM OF CONSCIOUSNESS

Throughout the rest of this book I'm going to pass along my knowledge as it relates to making a career in podcasting. Yes, I'm one of the "lucky" ones, but it didn't come easy. There were so many pitfalls along the way, so many lessons I had to learn the hard way. If podcasting was just about being the talent, many more would succeed at it, but in reality there is much more to it.

My shortcomings, when it comes to podcasting, have always been the technical end of things. At heart, my talent lies in my ability to create something out of nothing and then present that through an entertaining performance. Man, if that's all there was to it, how easy life would be. There's a whole other aspect when it comes to being successful in podcasting, and that is the technical end. Though you can probably figure out how to record a show, you then have to understand how to edit it, know how to upload it to the Internet, then you have to make clips from it, shorts, etc. Then there is understanding algorithms—which I STILL don't get after 10 years. There is a science to putting videos on YouTube—science I don't even know or understand: what color font should I use, what time of the day is best to post it, what are the keywords to use in the title, and don't forget those !@#$%^& hash tags.

I can't be bothered with that shit; my mind just isn't wired that way. And that's where you have to be super careful because you are going to have to bring people aboard to do all of that for you. But . . . those people will fail you 99 percent of the time. They'll start strong and leave with a whimper in less than three months. Reason being—they expect to make big dollars right away, and podcasting just doesn't work that way. It takes years of consistency, of being there and providing good, honest entertainment.

And there is just a danger when you give these people your passwords because now not only can they get into all your shit . . . but they can also lock you out of it. That happened to me on my Facebook page. I hired a guy to post clips of my shows, gave him all my passwords, and in the matter of a month he had locked me out, wanting cash from me to let me back in. This shit happens, and it will kill your business.

That's why I recommend if you are going to go in this field, you need to learn all aspects of it—everything. You can't rely on other people because people, in general, are just not reliable. As we speak, I just had another person quit posting edited videos on my YouTube channel simply because the amount he earned this month (based off percentages) was less than the money he earned last. Reality? If I quit podcasting because one month's income was lower than the previous month, I would have been out of business dozens of times.

Learn everything you possibly can, especially when it has your name on it. Don't rely on others—they will let you down and disappoint you 99 percent of the time.

51 THE "OFFICIAL" END OF PYRO AND BALLYHOO

Below is the original press release that I sent out to all my subscribers once I put the final kibosh on pyroandballyhoo.com:

UPDATE FROM VINCE (3/14/2015)

Dear Members of My Beloved Brand,

First, and foremost, I want to thank every, single one of you, who have supported me throughout this very difficult time. I want you to know that I have read every e-mail, tweet and Facebook post that you have sent, and your love, loyalty and dedication has moved me beyond words.

And, it was those very sentiments that helped me realize that I could never walk away from those who have made it possible for me to have a career in which I could support my family. I will forever be indebted to all of you.

With that, during my brief time away, I have been looking at every option that lies before me, that would not only suit my immediate family, but my extended family—you,

THE BRAND. I am so thankful that there are a host of others out there that appreciate what we do, and what we stand for. Being wanted is one of the greatest experiences anyone could ever want.

With all that being said, I am close to making an announcement as to where we will go from here as a family. I think it's very fair to say that will come within the next two weeks. However, before going forward—I must clear up the past one final time. I'm not going to go into detail here, because quite honestly I feel that isn't necessary. My focus is on looking ahead to what the future holds. A glance in the rear view mirror is only useful to help you in not repeating the same mistakes over.

About 10 months ago I was approached with a proposal to start my own website. The structure of that agreement was presented to me, which of course laid out the financials to the agreement. I agreed in principle to the arrangement that was put before me.

Over the next ten months, I honored all aspects of that agreement. I even went above and beyond what my financial responsibility was to that agreement. After a trip to Los Angeles, I was sent an e-mail by my associate where a new agreement was not only demanded, but an ultimatum was attached stating that he would "shut down" the site, if I didn't agree to his new terms.

At that point, I informed my associate that where I come from a man's word is his bond. I told him that I accepted an offer that he made to me 10 months ago, and that I had every intention to continue to honor that agreement. Forty-eight hours later—he locked me out of PyroandBallyhoo.com.

With that, I eliminated all my checking account information from the PyroandBallyhoo.com PayPal account, leaving no opportunity for anyone to say that I took one, single penny from the account once I realized that I was locked from the site. All that documentation is on record through PayPal.

That is the story. That is the way it unfolded. The loss has hurt me deeply, as I put every ounce of my blood, sweat and tears into PyroandBallyhoo.com, and never saw this coming. But . . . it came . . . I dealt with it . . . and now it's gone. At this point I'd like to thank my former associate for the effort he put in, and also wish him nothing but the best as he moves forward. Finally, anyone can choose to debate this for as long as they like, I have spoken my last word on the topic. Going forward, I am focused on one thing, and one thing only—what does all this mean for us—THE BRAND? Well, that answer will be revealed to all of you very shortly, as will the answer pertaining to those that may have lost a monthly payment to the site after I was locked out. Settling that issue has been a major priority for me, as I told you earlier on. So there you have it. I cannot tell you how excited I am concerning OUR new endeavor. As soon as the i's are dotted and the t's are crossed—you will all be the first to know. But for now. . . . I will leave you with this . . .

WE HAVE ONLY JUST BEGUN!!!

Peace,
Vince

52 THE BIRTH OF RUSSOSBRAND

Man, God had done it. Podcasting was what I was supposed to be doing. I was good at it, it was comfortable, and it was *me*! What's ironic is that once I did *Vicious Vincent's World of Wrestling*, back in 1991, I fell in love with radio. I never had this "dream" about working in the wrestling business and writing and producing television—I went down that path because I desperately needed a job at the time. But radio—that would have been my choice—that was my true love.

So, God gave me the next best thing—podcasting. However, I was in a bad spot. Again, being the content creator and talent, I needed someone who was going to be able to restore my site from a technical aspect. That's where God sent an angel my way. His name was Joe Locastro, it's like he appeared in the middle of the night, out of nowhere. At the time, I was in absolute panic mode not knowing what to do, but this godsend just showed up and got me up and running, retrieving months' worth of files that I had thought were lost when Mr. X locked me out of my only source of income.

Once the site was salvaged, I knew that I also needed some help running the day-to-day operations. A manager, so to speak, who had the ability to wear many hats. That's where I found Jeff "Jerry" Lane, who was a subscriber of pyroandballyhoo.com.

IMPORTANT NOTE:

Jeff Lane adopted the nickname Jerry thanks to my dad, who has a habit of butchering names. Yeah . . . I think that's where I got that gift from. Every day during our numerous daily calls, my dad will be trying to tell me about somebody, but at 94 years old, it's difficult for him to get names straight. And me, his cruel, cruel son, thinks that's hysterical, so I hop all over it once he opens that door.

Case in point: My father trying to tell me that former Atlanta Braves/ Chicago Cubs/Los Angeles Dodgers outfielder JASON HEYWARD got released:

Dad: "Hey, did you hear that Jason Howard got released by the Dodgers?"

Now, keep in mind, I know he's trying to say JASON HEYWARD.

Me: "Who?"

Dad: "Jason Howard, the outfielder for the Dodgers."

Me: "Moe Howard from the Three Stooges?"

Dad: "No, no, not Moe Howard—JASON Howard."

Me: "Jason Howard? Oh, you must mean Jason from *Friday the 13th*.

Dad: "NO—JASON HOWARD. The ballplayer!"

Me: "Oh, you mean Jason Giambi."

Dad: "No, no."

Then my dad will start going through the alphabet out loud, but to himself, somewhat like this:

Dad: "Jason . . . A . . . Allen, Adams . . . B . . . Bravo, Banks . . . C . . . Cooper. . . ."

Bro—he'll go through the whole alphabet.

Me: "He's a ballplayer?"

Dad: "Yeah, yeah, Jason Howard."

Me: "Oh, you mean Jason Bay, the retired outfielder of the Pirates?"

This will go on for 15 minutes at a clip like this.

Here are my dad's top three name changes of all time:

Jerry Lane (Jeff Lane)
Ti Kwan (Tony Khan)
Jack Flick (John Wick)

Ironically, I had a few things in common with Jeff that I didn't even know at the time. For starters, he spent some time living in Evansville, Indiana,

Amy's hometown and the place where I went to college for three years (and later moved back to for eight months—we'll get to that later). Also—he actually roomed with Dan Engler, aka Rudy Charles, former TNA referee, now senior WWE referee. Did you know that Rudy didn't know that mocha was chocolate? That's another story for another time.

Jeff seemed really committed. He was a wrestling fan, but not a mark, and had some experience writing for an indy promotion in Evansville. But, honestly, at the time, his resume didn't matter to me. I just needed a warm body, figuring he would just powder in a couple of months like Mr. X did.

With Jeff's help, we started the rebuild, and it started with a name change, to wash away the stank that Mr. X had brought upon Pyro and Ballyhoo in its final days.

53 THE ORIGIN OF THE NAME RUSSOSBRAND

How the name RussosBrand originated is an entertaining story. Being new on social media, I had no idea what I was doing. Was I posting too much, not enough, saying the right thing, the wrong thing—WHO KNEW? I was like a kid with a new toy where some assembly was required, who couldn't quite figure out the instructions to put the damn thing together. Over the years I have learned to master X (or Twitter), but back in those virgin days—I'm sure I was coming across as a mark.

So one day, I tweeted out something that got my good friend Taz hot. Now, for the record—I freakin' love Taz! And it's not hard to understand why. I *mark out* for characters, always have, always will. Just look at my timeline: Tom Jones, Tiny Tim, KISS, Tenacious D, John Wick (Jack Flick), Caesar of *Planet of the Apes* fame, Sebastian Maniscalco, "Elegant" Elliot Offen (see Howard Stern) . . . the list is endless.

Taz, to me, is the character of all characters. He just exemplifies everything that a Long Islander represents—sense of humor, sarcasm, attitude, chip on his shoulder, never wrong, loud, cocky, arrogant, opinionated, always right, prideful, and will fight you even on just a crooked look.

Now, I don't even remember what it was I put out there, but it aggravated Taz. So, Taz let it be known publicly, on social media, that he was a bit upset with his boy. What he said was something of the following—I paraphrase: "Now, I understand that you are trying to build your BRAND, and get your BRAND over, but it's too much." Up until that point, I didn't even understand what a "brand" actually was. So I looked at that, chuckled a bit because it was so Taz, and thought, "*that's it*: RUSSOSBRAND!" And the name stuck.

54 THE RELM NETWORK

With Jeff being the Robin to my Batman, the two of us were able to start rebuilding the newly minted RussosBrand. We did this mostly through being consistent. That is the key to becoming good at anything. That goes all the way back to my WWE Attitude Era days, where the shows had to be good, week after week . . . matter of fact, this week's show has to be better than last week's. That's how it starts—commitment to consistency and improvement.

Over time, we started to build a subscriber base of loyal, paying customers. I never went on that "free with ads" market, for a couple of reasons. 1) I didn't care about how many "hits" my podcast would get—to me, it's not a popularity contest, it's about how much money will I earn. Many people get caught up in the clicks, the views, the downloads—I never have. I'm interested in that loyal fan base that is going to support me through thick and thin—which the Brand does. 2) One of my favorite lines from one of my favorite movies, *Do the Right Thing*: pizzeria owner Sal says to his employee Mookie, "'Free'? There's no 'free' here!" That's right, there is no free. I don't work for free, and you shouldn't work for free either. All of our time is valuable—there is a worth to it. When I am working, I want to get PAID. America, bro. America.

When you look back at the Brand's history, you will see a slow but steady climb. Things didn't happen overnight; they won't in podcasting. That's why you see so many people come in and go out, especially in the wrestling genre. Former wrestlers think they're going to make money immediately—and when they don't, they're gone. We took steps, baby steps, realizing that we were investing in our future.

When I say that the Brand is a family—I truly mean that. Many of us know each other on a personal level—that has developed over years. And because of that, we are always looking out for each other, and it was thanks to a Brand member that the platform got its first major break.

One day, I got an email from a subscriber telling me that I should look into this fairly new venture called the RELM Network. They were a small podcasting station out of the Baltimore, Maryland, area. In doing business, I think it's smart to take a step through every door—you just never know what's inside. So that's what I did. It was there where I met Marc Ronick and had a productive and informative first conversation with him.

The RELM Network was a podcasting channel with a variety of different shows, many based around comedy. At the time there was actually one wrestling show on the network—and I will get to that later. Signing on with RELM would basically mean that they would get a percentage of our subscribers, and they in turn would run everything for us—all Jeff and I would have to do would be provide the content. This is exactly what we needed, *especially* when it came to customer care and customer service. Jeff and I were a two-man team, and we just didn't have the time to deal with technical problems and so forth.

After a few solid conversations, Marc sent me a contract, which I immediately signed, and we were now in business together. This was the first step of our growth.

Oh, yeah, the other wrestling podcast on RELM.

Prior to signing with RELM, they were already home to another wrestling podcast. Upon my signature on the paper, Marc asked me if I wouldn't mind making an appearance on their show. I said no problem, we're all a family now—right? Wrong. I went on the show, and it was pretty clear, pretty quickly that the two hosts of the show were dirt sheet marks. Of course, while I was on the show, they treated me cordially, but once the show ended, they went into "wrestling marks hate Vince Russo" mode—because that is what they're required to do by the other wrestling marks who hate Vince Russo—and started thrashing and burying me. They went as far as to suggest my wife's a whore. Much credit to Marc, as he would eventually send those guys packing.

55 AN ASSIST FROM STONE COLD

The relationship with Marc and RELM Network was another godsend and an integral part of our success. We were building a loyal following, but still not quite reaching the masses. When it comes to podcasting, I have to laugh. My adversaries all love to point out, "Russo doesn't have the numbers that Cornette or Bischoff have—he's a nobody." Yeah, but let's keep in mind—I was a writer! Do you know how many years Bischoff and Cornette had weekly exposure on national television? I was on the boob tube for literally a hiccup! So that's why comments like that never bothered me. I just wanted to grow my audience to make Jeff and myself more money. I never looked at podcasting as a popularity contest.

I'm grinding, whatever I can do to get the Brand out to even one more person. And, here we go again, if you think God isn't conducting this orchestra then WHO the !@#$%^& is?!?! Out of nowhere, I get a DM on Twitter from an old friend, "Stone Cold" Steve Austin. At the time, Steve had the most successful wrestling podcast on the *planet* on PodcastOne. Steve invited me to be a guest on his show, and without hesitation I jumped at the opportunity because not only am I Steve's number-one fan, but what this would do for my brand was invaluable.

So I went on Steve's show, and it was a huge success. I think Steve was especially thrilled with it because I was being completely honest about everything. I wasn't walking a line, afraid of whom I may or may not piss off in the wrestling industry because I had zero incentive to try to be in favor with anybody. Having just come off that TNA nightmare, the last thing I was looking for was a ticket back into professional wrestling—I was a hundred-percent in the Vince Russo Business.

That's why I don't interview wrestlers on my show anymore, where I used to do an interview every week. I found that most of them were just full of shit; not sincere at all. They never said what they really want to say, for fear of pissing off a Vince McMahon (back then) or whoever else was in charge at the time. They always wanted to keep that door open for an appearance, the WWE Hall of Fame invite, a legends deal, or that one last run. And, from a business standpoint, that was smart of them—I didn't blame them—but on the Brand, I just didn't want the bullshit—I had no use for it.

Following our interview, after we were off the air, Steve and I had a personal chat, and he asked me how things were going. I told Steve things were going well, but slow. I just had to figure out a way to get RussosBrand out there. At that point, Steve said, "Well, hell, why don't you just do a show on PodcastOne? That will get you out there."

Are you !@#$%^& me? I wasn't even thinking along those lines, because never would I have put Steve in that spot where I would ask such a favor from him—you just don't do that to people, especially friends. But now he was suggesting it! God—cue the blaring trumpets!

It was only a matter of days before I got a call from the head of PodcastOne, and within weeks I had a show on their network. This was unbelievable! I could have never done this on my own, and I was so grateful and thankful to Steve. At that time, PodcastOne was the big dawg in podcasting, and now Vince Russo—writer—had a show on their platform.

So, the formula would be simple, do our flagship show on PodcastOne, to let people know what we were all about, then send them to RussosBrand for additional shows and content. In other words, the PodcastOne show would be the catalyst for us to make money on the Brand through subscriptions. I knew the PodcastOne show wasn't going to be the moneymaker, because I just didn't have the name, or the pull, of a "Stone Cold" to bring in the masses.

56 CASTRATING THE MARKS

At this point, I was becoming a content-making machine, recording several shows daily, each one with a different theme. But what I was lacking was a "flagship" show—one that would be synonymous with RussosBrand. Then it dawned on me, why not do a show wrapped around my favorite subject, a world I was introduced to in 1991. Why don't I do a show called . . . "*Exposing the Dirt Sheet Marks*"? Yeah—but I don't want to just expose them, I want to cut their balls off! After that thought, "*Castrating the Marks*" popped into my head. So *Castrating the Marks* was incepted.

STREAM OF CONSCIOUSNESS

I am ALWAYS getting asked, "Vince, by your definition . . . what is a 'wrestling M=mark'?" Let me explain. To understand, you have to know the origin of the word "mark" in this context. Many, many moons ago when carnivals were popular, a customer would walk into one of those game booths—let's say the "Softball in the Milk Can" (that would be one of those huge antique milk containers with handles on both sides, with an opening on top—a bit bigger than a softball). The customer would spend tens upon twenties (dollars), trying to toss a softball through an opening that it could hardly fit through to win a cheap prize. Once the barker took a person's money, he then gave him a slap on the back—with his hand covered in talcum powder—to mark the customer so the runners of other carnival games could identify him: this was a *money mark*. That's where it derived from.

Over the years the term "mark" has been somewhat watered down. Today, if you are referred to as a mark, it means you are a huge fan of something or someone and you give them, or it, your full support. For example, if you champion a singer, actor, professional sports figure, sports team, TV show, fictional character, movie franchise, etc., and you dig deep in your pockets to support them—you would be considered a mark. You buy everything they are selling: albums, T-shirts, hats, posters, calendars, DVDs, you name it—as in, "If Taylor Swift's name is on it, I'm buying it!" Thus, you are spending all your money on that individual, brand, company, whatever—so you're now categorized as being a money mark.

And, let me first say, I am a money mark for numerous things. If you entertain me, I have no problem supporting you monetarily, as a matter of fact I want to. Over the years, here's a list of the baker's dozen of things I'm a money mark for that comes to mind:

Rihanna
Tenacious D
Steve Perry
Tiny Tim
Planet of the Apes
"Elegant" Elliot Offen
albums
hippies
Rocky
San Francisco Giants
KISS
John Wick
The Honeymooners

Off the list:

Howard Stern

Man, what a disappointment Howard Stern turned out to be. I started listening to Stern in 1983, before I got married. I first found him on WNBC, and I was totally hooked. He was my true inspiration for wanting to get into radio. He exemplified the most important things to me—saying whatever he wanted, whenever he wanted, unedited, no matter the consequences and not giving a !@#$%^& what anybody thought.

But at some point everything changed. At first, I wrote it off to Howard mellowing as he got a bit older, but then he got to a point of ridiculousness where I just couldn't defend him anymore. I don't know if the guy just wanted to hobnob with only celebrity A-listers, or he was being controlled by the Illuminati, or he made a deal with the Devil, but whatever the case—my hero sold out.

So yeah, that list of 13 . . . I've spent a ton of money on those over the years, even though KISS lost some favor with me as well when they made the decision to put Ace's and Peter's makeup on the impostors who replaced them.

The definition of a *wrestling mark*, however, is completely different. Here is how you know you are a wrestling mark:

- You have convinced yourself that professional wrestling is REAL.
- Professional Wrestling is THE MOST IMPORTANT THING in your entire life.
- You own A LOT of black shirts with PIT STAINS.
- You don't just want to GO to a wrestling show, you want to be a PART of it.
- You sing along with wrestlers' theme songs at the top of your lungs.
- Dave Meltzer is your GOD.
- "WORK RATE" in FAKE Wrestling Matches is IMPORTANT to you.
- You HATE any form of entertainment in your wrestling.
- You ORGASM over Japanese wrestling.
- You are opposed to seeing attractive women in wrestling.
- You walk around the arena with a championship belt over your shoulder.
- You live rent free in YOUR MOM'S BASEMENT.
- You are part of a "tribe" that loves one wrestling brand and hates the other wrestling brand.

- You hate Vince Russo.
- You are offended if anyone refers to you as a MARK.
- You HONESTLY believe Triple H or Tony Khan are "TRUE" Bookers of the Year.
- You cried when Cody Rhodes finished his "story" and beat Roman Reigns at *WrestleMania*.
- You make EVERY EXCUSE IN THE BOOK when your brand's rating is down for the week.

If you fall under *any* of the above categories, you are indeed a WRESTLING MARK.

But getting back to *Castrating the Marks* . . .

Yeah, man, from the first time I was introduced to that world through John Arezzi back in 1991, the dirt sheet media was always an aspect of the business that to me served no purpose and hurt the business much more than it helped it. Not only by publishing spoilers, where you would tell your audience what was going to happen before it happened, but also the effect it had on some people working in the business via negative reports or false rumors and narratives driven by personal agendas for certain gain.

I just could never stand these people. Again, I think the underlying cause of that was because they all convinced themselves that they were something they *were not*. How can you be an insider when you aren't even allowed anywhere near a locker room and have no working knowledge of a business you were actually never in?

Yeah, this show was going to expose them for the frauds they were, by playing audio and video clips from their own podcasts and sharing some of their tweets from their X accounts. But to be clear, the objective was not to hate them through vigor, but to make fun of them through comedy. It was going to be a light-hearted show where we would showcase just how silly and incompetent these people were. I also believed that if they watched this show, they themselves would realize how much of their lives they were spending on something that did not matter, perhaps forcing them to rethink their priorities.

This is one of the most quotable lines I think I've ever come up with: "If you're putting your priority on things that don't matter, you're neglecting the things that do."

And, why do I say that? I say it because I myself was guilty of that when I worked for Vince and the WWF. There was a time when that company was my main priority, and I put my family on the back burner. I am so regretful when stating that, but it is the truth . . . and I'm ashamed of it. Thank God I got smacked upside the head with a dose of reality when Vince told me, "Hire a nanny to watch your kids"—that was the call that woke me up. By the time I went over to WCW in September of 1999, my obsession to succeed . . . was now simply a job to support my family.

Unfortunately, the one thing I didn't count on was the fact that none of these dirt sheet assclowns have a sense of humor. They take the wrestling business and their part in it so seriously that they don't have the ability to ever laugh at themselves.

This is what would cost me my show on PodcastOne.

57 MR. Y GETS ME CANCELED FROM PODCASTONE

So, we launch *Castrating the Marks*, and from the jump it's a great success. Our subscription base is really enjoying the show and its originality, comedy, and the foolishness in the way we go about presenting the dirt sheet assclowns. And we are producing it with the exact intent that I shared in the former chapter—in a light-hearted fashion with no anger or hatred involved.

When we record *Castrating the Marks*, Jeff gets all the submissions directly from the Brand: they send him content throughout the entire week, then he gathers it, picks what he believes is the best material, then presents it to me. Until then, I have NO IDEA what's on the show for that week, so when I see it and analyze it, I'm experiencing it for the first time.

On this particular show, Jeff shows me a picture of a certain former dirt sheet hack—whose real name I refuse to use in fear of corroding or staining the pages of this book, while also giving him the Vince Russo "rub"—so I will refer to him to as Mr. Y. Now, you may find this hard to believe, but Mr. Y and I actually started our relationship on good terms. At the time, he was starting a new wrestling podcast, and I offered to have him come on my show for some free pub. The reason I did that was because the guy was coming from some level of success working the Hollywood celebrity beat, so I figure his approach in the wrestling world would be a more entertaining one.

Mr. Y and I hit it off on that first show, and it was as I expected, funny and light-hearted. Mr. Y shared some of his Hollywood stories, which I marked out for—it was great stuff. A few weeks later, I would make some comments on my show, it was either about an incident I had at the Atlanta airport or some comments I made about my Christian beliefs. It was one of those two . . . or maybe both. Little did I know, but Mr. Y was a lefty, a liberal, somebody with an agenda that would just look to castrate you if you were on the "other side." I was oblivious to this. I'm not a political guy, frankly; I really don't give a shit—never have.

This is where I learned all about "cancel culture" I had no idea there even was such a thing. The concept is simple: If you don't agree with my opinions, beliefs, or ideas, I will go full-out attack mode on your ass, saying anything and everything imaginable to make sure that your livelihood comes to an end and you can no longer support your family or yourself. That's cancel culture.

So, now Mr. Y starts making some public comments about me, basically labeling me a "racist" and a "sexist." Yeah, they love that shit. When you have an opposing viewpoint from theirs, they start with the *labels*—a sure sign you're dealing with the lowest common denominator.

Anyway, I catch wind of this, and I DM Mr. Y, asking him, "What the !@#$%^&."

From there, without reason, this namby-pamby sissy Mary girlie man started spouting off with some self-righteous bullshit. Needless to say, it got ugly fast. Now, you have to understand these dirt sheet rectums—you have to be smarter than them, always one step ahead. In a situation like this, what they are trying to do is bait you. They're trying to provoke you into saying something you might regret later—so they can run with it publicly. So every time you find yourself in a situation like that with one of these dirt sheet anuses, you have to immediately go to the mindset that they may be recording your conversation. As soon as I realized this may be the case, I was the one who fed Mr. Y that bait that he swallowed without realizing it.

At one point during our DM exchange, Mr. Y—just as I thought he would—threatened to go public with our online dialogue. Knowing this would be his move, I was prepared and beat him to the punch by sharing it myself because the exchange was detrimental to him, not me. This not only exposed him, but it embarrassed him . . . and when you embarrass one of these freaks, they go all-out Karen on you.

So now Mr. Y was on full alert. Tracking everything I did and said, just looking for that one opportunity to pounce on it and cancel me. I have to admit, I never expected him to go to the level that he did—the lowest of the lowest scum buckets—but he did. Yeah, I guess I underestimated him, but as it turned out it was all for the best.

While Mr. Y was looking for something on me, RussosBrand is returning the favor. They are tracking this dirty rag with more precision than Detective Columbo once he gets a hunch!!! Within only a matter of days, a submission for *Castrating* was sent in. What was submitted was a picture of Mr. Y and his girlfriend wearing Halloween masks—somewhat disturbing ones—and kissing. That was it—all I needed. A picture with both their faces fully covered. I ran with this: "Well, at least his girlfriend makes him put on a mask before she kisses him" . . . etc. See—light-hearted humor.

As expected, Y goes ballistic—BALLISTIC, I tell ya, over a Halloween picture where nobody's face is even revealed. Man, when I tell you what followed, it will sound so familiar. There is a playbook with these dimwits, one they go to over and over and over again. According to Mr. Y, because I showed that picture, his girlfriend is now getting threatening emails and tweets. What? Are you !@#$%^& kidding me? Are you really going to play that card? So I ask him through a DM to send me the emails and the tweets, because if this were indeed true, I told him I would contact those Brand members myself and tell them to cease their actions. Of course . . . he never sent anything—they simply didn't exist.

Now, after I've called him out—they hate when you do that—he has to up his game, so the narrative takes a slight turn. After failing to present any evidence by way of DMs, texts, or emails, the story changes and becomes I am now inciting and ordering the Brand Army to go after his girlfriend. Remember, I don't even know this woman. What a hundred-percent bona-fide !@#$%^&WAD!!!

But it gets better.

Now, the dopey dweeb directs all his followers to contact PodcastOne and tell them that Vince Russo is encouraging his listeners to troll, attack, and threaten an innocent female. You have to keep in mind that this is the height of cancel culture. It was literally only a day or two later that I received this email:

> From: garyy****@xxxxx.com
> To: vincerusso@xxxxx.com
> Cc: normp*****@xxxxx.com; jimb***@xxxxx.com; gregb*****@xxxxx.com; kitg***@xxxxx.com; chrisd******@xxxxx.com; elid******@xxxxx.com; alt********@xxxxx.com
> Sent: Wed, Mar 21, 2018, 7:41 a.m.
> Subject: Cancellation Notice
>
> Hi Vince—
>
> I regret to inform you that we are providing you with Notice pursuant to paragraph 4 of our March 19, 2016 agreement that we will be cancelling your podcast effective April 20, 2018. If you wish to stop producing episodes prior to that date, we will not take exception. Notify Chris D******, who is cc'd above if you want to stop production before the 20th. You will continue to receive statements and payments until your billings have been collected or determined to be uncollectable. Please feel free to reach out to me if you have any questions.
>
> Best regards,
> Gary

No shit—literally within a day or two.

When I email them back and asked for the reasoning behind this prompt decision, here was their response:

> From: garyy****@xxxxx.com
> To: vincerusso@xxxxx.com
> Cc: chrisd*****@xxxxx.com
> Sent: Wed, Mar 21, 2018, 11:52 a.m.
> Subject: RE: Cancellation Notice

> Vince—paragraph 4 doesn't require a reason on our part, but since you asked, your shows have included adverse comments about women and ethnic groups that have resulted in advertisers not wanting to be associated with your podcast.
>
> Gary

When I asked them if they could supply me with the "adverse comments" they were talking about, they didn't—again, because there were none. PodcastOne simply canceled my show because a bunch of marks contacted them with false claims pertaining to a woman—Mr. Y's girlfriend.

After that email, I was able to get the head of PodcastOne on the phone. I'm sorry, I don't remember his name. But I asked him, Did you even look into these claims made by Mr. Y? Did you even take one second to see if there was any truth whatsoever pertaining to his charges? They didn't, and they hadn't. At one point in the conversation, Steve got brought up—remember? "Stone Cold" got me the gig. Now, I had to be very careful here, I certainly wasn't going to drag Steve into this, whether it meant saving the show or not.

I get the impression that those making the decision to cancel my show hadn't put two and two together and didn't realize that the guy with the number-one show on their network was the same guy who put in a word for me. Once they figured that out—they certainly didn't want to upset Steve—so they started backtracking, telling me that they could put me back on the air, but they weren't going to guarantee me any amount of income. At that point, I simply just said, "You guys should be ashamed of yourselves. For you to act in such a cowardly fashion, listening to somebody blatantly trying to put me out of business without even looking into it . . . I really don't think I want to have anything to do with your network at this point."

And that was it. My first experience with the power of cancel culture . . . little did I know it would be far from the last.

SIDE NOTE:

It was sometime later that Mr. Y accused me once again of making a disparaging remark about his girlfriend—again, a woman I didn't even know. Having heard enough of his bullshit, I was actually able to get in contact with her. During our email exchange, she said that whatever the comment was that I made at the time, she knew that it was nothing defamatory or slanderous towards her. We had a nice, civil discussion, after which I never heard from Mr. Y again.

58 GOD AT IT AGAIN

Man, this was a blow, a massive hit. It's not that we were generating a lot of income at PodcastOne, that was going to happen over time, but the loss of the exposure on such a well-known platform—that was going to sting.

But, again, that's where God comes in. Remember I told you that God made it clear to me that he knew what I needed? Well, there was such backlash over the way Mr.Y screwed me over at PodcastOne that many of those who were listening to the show FREE on that platform were now coming over to RussosBrand and subscribing in droves! We practically doubled our subscriber base, and that increase alone generated more income than what I was making at PodcastOne. Man, I would have never called that one; I guess I underestimated my audience. They knew I got screwed over, they knew the claims were bogus, and they were going to stand by me and show their total support on a financial level. It was a blessing in disguise, and something that Mr. Y never could have considered.

So now we were rolling. I was in the best position I'd been in for years—physically, mentally, spiritually, and financially. RussosBrand was starting to become lucrative, and it represented an arena where I had the absolute freedom to be myself. Free of any of the Corporate Bullshit that I had been forced to deal with for so many years.

Thank you, Jesus! And thank you, Mr. Y!

59 RUSSOSBRAND FULL-TIME GIG

It took a couple of years to get there, but RussosBrand eventually became a full-time job, supporting Amy and me. I'd be lying if I said it was an easy road, because it wasn't. The first two years, I barely made enough to get by, but never did the thought cross my mind—not even once—to quit. This truly was my dream job, the best job I'd ever have in my life. It was such a freeing feeling, to finally be allowed to just be me—no handcuffs, no restrictions, no politics . . . I was free of all that bullshit that comes basically with any corporate job. I clearly was one of the lucky ones.

Always giving credit where it's due, I have to prop up Jeff Lane. Jeff has been there for me from day one. Yeah, we've had our disagreements, and some arguments if you want me to be totally honest, but what superseded it all was his loyalty. And that's something I demand. If I'm loyal to you, I expect the same in return. Jeff has never screwed me—it's just not in him to do so—and I can never thank him enough for that.

We produced many shows on RussosBrand, and the beauty of it was that they were all with friends from the business. Aside from the hundreds of current and former wrestlers that I've interviewed, the following had their own shows on the network: ODB, the Beautiful People's Angelina Love and Velvet Sky, Justin Credible, Taeler Hendrix, Goldy Locks, Al Snow, EC3,

Stevie Ray, Disco Inferno, Stevie Richards, and Bin Hamin. These were all people that I truly loved—good people—it's no wonder that we're all on the outside looking in. I've said to this day, "It's hard to be a good person and work in the wrestling business." Nothing could be more the truth than that.

Speaking of family, that's what many of our subscribers became. I'm talking about Troy, Potts, Lacey, Michael Krause, Chris "The Hun" Pyhtila, John Schlegel, Rev. Buddy Green, Dimitrios, Ross, Carl Gray, the late great "Hit Man," Mike Durband, Laura, Scott Smith, CJ, Cpbstation, Large Larry, Jack Nicholas, DougieV, FinalBoss, Francesco Castano, Nathan Vaughan, Gabe Tough, Frank Kersh, Brandon Stransky, Mdot, "Tribal Chief" Darren Ellington, Miss Chantelle, Jay Bacca, NoDQ Virtue, Matthew Ortiz, Gooner CestLaVie, Scott Ward, Anders Ong, Dimitri Hondros, Reverend Smily, AnnaLaura, the late great Jared Cantatore, Philly Dan, Brent Logan, Coach Steve Cully, Nelson Martinez, Steve Solet, Cazz, John Dawson, Matt DiVenti, Peter Bahi, Lucky Da Truth, dman, Clive, Stephanie, LyinRatin, Michael Desrochers, Chris Cortes, Charles Redman, Baron von Lector, "Large" Larry Egner, Kevin Mari, Evil Jackalopes, ManDeer, Tasha Garner, Ivan Batista, J12, Chris Naes, Greg O Grady, Ash Goodin, Andrew Lee Starke, BboyWill, Nicholas Look, Adge Groucott, Matthew Chmura, Arturo Gonzalez III, Baker Runge, NinjaGreg, Matthew Maloney, Josh Heggs, Dimitri Hondros, Boris Kaiser, Rita Coughlin, Kevin Kimmins, Mark Martucci, Harvey Bright, Elrod, Joel Diamond, Adrian Willis, TrueStorey, Pat Cusick, Brandon Brooks, Ryan Wilson, Stewart Cowles, Scott Eagan, Matt Swift, Dr. Funkenstein, Brian Adams, Jeff Barrett, "Best of" Joel, Daniel Aldape, Gabor Nagy, Sean Burgess, Willgaby Gonzalez, JerMaJesty, Leon Cardin, and man, way, way too many others to mention.

Everything was going as smoothly as it possible could, too good to be true, who's going to toss in that monkey wrench—somebody has got to !@#$%^& this thing up, right?

Right.

Well, despite all the usual suspects, it ended up being RELM Network.

60 RELM CLOSES ITS DOORS

Over the course of the next three years, things were running as smoothly as possible with RussosBrand. The effort I was putting forward in front of the camera Jeff was mirroring behind it. When it comes to scheduling, meeting deadlines, and managing time, Jeff is as much committed to doing what it takes as yours truly. That speaks volumes, as the process is nonstop. Every day, there is something that must be done. In podcasting, it's always about living up to your commitment; when your subscribers are expecting a show on Monday at noon, it needs to be there Monday at noon—they are waiting for it. The second it's late, you are getting dozens of emails. Jeff is never late. Never. Sure, I wish at times he was a bit more motivated, but his absolute hardlined structure has been vital—one of the keys of our success.

There was another disappointment during that timeframe, where I was given the opportunity to go on Westwood One, and work with former senior vice president of *The Howard Stern Show* Tim Sabean. Tim had become aware of me through his dealings with Bruce Prichard, and after having a couple of phone conversations, he decided to give me a shot on his platform. Westwood One was the competitor to PodcastOne, so this was another shot to get RussosBrand to the masses.

Here's Vince "Pathological Liar" Russo talking. We didn't draw, man, we just didn't draw. Can you imagine me admitting that? There were some big hitters on that network, and we just couldn't hang on a numbers perspective. Again, just to remind everybody, I was mainly a writer/producer in the wrestling business—something that many in the entertainment industry look down upon—and despite all that, I had still parlayed it into a 25-year career. However, we were niche. We had a loyal following, but we were never going to go mainstream.

Think about it—the casual wrestling fans and television viewers who enjoyed my work weren't on social media talking about wrestling every day. They weren't going to wrestling websites or listening to wrestling podcasts. They were normal people, with normal lives, normal jobs, and normal priorities (among which pro wrestling was not one). I knew that, and I understood that. We were always going to have a solid foundation and following, but we were never going to have even AEW reach.

The cool thing about Tim Sabean was that he called me and shot straight with me. There was no bullshit, no beating around the bush, and I greatly respected him for that. It was an experiment that didn't work, and that was OK.

STREAM OF CONSCIOUSNESS

It tickles me to death when I hear the Vince Russo Haters declare, "Russo takes credit for everything successful, but the failures are never his fault." What an absolute bullshit narrative. That's the spin they love to spew. For starters, I love giving credit to others, and I love putting people over. That's all people want, a nice pat on the back, an attaboy, you did a great job. Man, commending someone on their idea or hard work, it just gives them such a great feeling of joy and pride—why wouldn't you do that? Plus—It's free. It costs you nothing. This is the third book I've written; I dare you to go back and read how many people I've put over along the way. I just put Tim Sabean over for giving us the axe from Westwood One.

Now, on the other side of that, I might love failure even more. You think that sounds nuts? It's not at all. With failure comes growth. You need to fail in order to succeed. When you accept that throughout your lifetime you are going to have hundreds, thousands, maybe even millions of misses, you start understanding two things: 1) It is impossible to win every time. Unless you're God Almighty Himself, you're going to take some Ls. And, 2) There is a reason that you lost. Whatever that disappointment—what it sprang from wasn't supposed to happen. Many times this is the case because you are chasing your own passions . . . and not God's. Think about it, if God is writing your story, then it's going to be *his* story and not yours. So, I believe when you fail, there is a message in that disappointment. Why did I fail? What is God trying to tell me? What am I taking away from this?

When you read the bible, you will understand that everything that happens in your lifetime is designed to bring you closer to God. Once you have a thorough understanding of that, then a "failure" is not a failure at all, it's a win. How can you deem anything in life a disappointment if it is going to make your bond with God stronger? That cannot be measured as a negative! That makes zero sense. When you turn your life over to him, you just start seeing everything through a positive lens. There is meaning and a message in everything. That's how he changes us from the inside out.

I'd be lying—again—if I told you I saw this one coming . . . I never did.

It was May 2021, the Brand was running as smoothly and sufficiently as possible. Safe to say we were a well-oiled machine at that point. Our customer base was strong, and Jeff and I were both making a living. Thinking that the pothole-infested road was behind us, out of the blue I get a call from Marc Ronick: "Vince, my partner and I are moving out of podcasting to pursue other opportunities, so we plan on shutting down RELM." Just like that. There were no warning signs, not even a hint of such a bombshell. I was caught totally off guard. I didn't even really understand what that meant for the Brand at that time. RELM took care of everything for us, with the most important thing being the system in which the subscribers paid for our service. I knew absolutely nothing about that—zilch.

In looking at my options at the time, I couldn't afford for RELM to just close its doors. Through all the turmoil that RussosBrand had overcome, Marc and RELM Network had been the anchor that kept us grounded. Now, I wasn't going to attempt to talk Marc out of his dreams and aspirations, so I had to figure something out. I couldn't start from scratch—we had come so far already.

To me, there was only one solution, and that was to buy RELM Network myself. That way, part of the agreement could be for Marc to take a few months to teach me how the entire operation worked—getting payments from subscribers, tech support, which vendors provided what, etc. Marc agreed, and he turned his company over to me at a very reasonable cost.

Marc lived up to his part of the agreement, but in the transition . . . a huge problem came to the surface. In the last few months of doing business with RELM, a third party from China was hacking into our system and directing our subscription money into their bank account!

What the fuck?! Yeah, man, another f-bomb.

At that point, Marc recommended to me that we have somebody rebuild RELM Network's site, turning it into a new system that would be free of and secure from hackers. It's not like I had any choice—this was something I was going to have to do immediately. Unfortunately, now the reasonable price at which Marc offered RELM to me . . . was going to expand by at least ten grand.

I had to do it; I just didn't have any alternatives. On the bright side—now, since a new programmer was going to develop a whole new site for us, I had the opportunity to change the look and the name. So, in the rebuild, RELM Network became Channel Attitude. Yeah, man, the name wasn't a difficult one to come up with, and neither was the concept. I wanted to create a network where I could bring on dozens, if not hundreds, of new and existing podcasts under one roof. Channel Attitude was going to become both a content creator and a major source of all content for all people . . . left, right, and middle, didn't matter—we were going to have something for everybody—at least, that was the plan.

Marc recommended a programmer to us who was familiar with a system called DAP, which was vital to our site. DAP allows you to use both Stripe and PayPal as options for subscribers to pay you. Unfortunately, what Marc didn't know at the time was that DAP was the way our hacker found his way into our system.

After speaking to the programmer that Marc suggested—let's call him Mr. Z, I hired him for the job. Now, keep in mind, I hired him with a completed amount given to me of around $10K; Mr. Z would bill me at an hourly rate of $100, which I thought was an exorbitant amount—but no big deal because I'm still looking at the final number of $10K . . . right?

So Mr. Z starts working on the site, and billing me every week:

Week 1: $2,000
Week 2: $2,000
Week 3: $2,500

Man—only three weeks, and we are getting close to that $10K, aren't we?

A month in, and Mr. Z goes well past the $10K mark without an end in sight.

Little did I know at the time, but that was the least of my worries.

As things are starting to get extremely dicey between me and Mr. Z over the money, we have much, much bigger issues. We now discover that we have a new hacker. How did we discover this? Well, one night Jeff and I were both on the new site, and Mr. Hacker pops in and starts deleting everything as we watched helplessly.

Immediately, we call Mr. Z, only to find that he doesn't have a clue what to do—I mean—not a !@#$%^& clue. And, yes, our beloved hacker was getting into our system through DAP, just like our ol' Chinese friend did. Man, we are totally screwed at this point. I don't know what to do. Remembering my lawyer's Rolodex of who's who, I once again call Frank, to see if he has anyone who might be able to help us. Frank refers me to a new programmer—and the process begins all over again.

Being that there was no way to get around the DAP problem, the new programmer had to basically start from scratch. So, yeah, I had to pay Mr. Z for literally nothing but his time, and now I was going to be into a new programmer for yet another five figures.

Man, it took the new programmer literal months to get us back up and running. During that time, we were able to keep most of our subscribers, but due to the chaos, it was almost impossible to recruit new ones and generate more income. In other words, I kept pumping more money in, while less and less was coming out.

SIDE NOTE:

Do you know that the hacker had the balls to email me and not only take credit for !@#$%^& up our entire site, but he also took the time to show me just how he did it?? Man, what a nice guy!

The new programmer finally got us up and running again after an agonizing long time. We wound up parting ways with him for yet a third programmer when we realized that tech support was not his priority. I couldn't have our subscribers wait a week, or two, to have their tickets answered. The dude was a nice guy, and I try to stay in touch with him to this day, but he just had some personal issues that were more important for him to resolve.

The money I spent, when all was said and done, was easily over $50,000. That was just the cost to stay in business. I've never recouped that money, but I was never going to let RussosBrand die . . . I loved it too much. Whatever it took, I knew I was going to have to find the money . . . and I did. But again, it was the true passion I felt for what I was doing that pushed me through—that same passion that I once had for professional wrestling/sports entertainment.

Key word being ONCE.

61 I HATE PRO WRESTLING

It's hard for me, at 64, to comprehend that I once had a passion for professional wrestling; not an obsession . . . a passion. From an early age, maybe 10 or 11, wrestling was something that I really enjoyed. I remember the first time I came across it on UHF, the first show I went to at the Commack Arena, the first *WrestleMania* where you could only see it on closed-circuit television in a movie theater. And I remember these moments fondly and vividly; seeing a beaten and bloodied Bruno come back every time, Spiros Arion shoving Chief's traditional headdress down his gullet, Hulk winning the world title at MSG for the first time, *Rock 'n' Wrestling* on MTV, the André the Giant/Hulk Hogan "ripping of the cross," Macho Man feeling the wrath of a venomous snake tearing into his skin, "The Barber Shop" where Shawn Michaels was made, etc., etc., etc. All these moments are sharp, clear, enjoyable, and most importantly . . . memorable.

That passion stayed with me all the way through my work at WWF. I loved what I was doing during that time, and I really felt I was keeping the memory of Vince Sr. alive through the creation of legendary characters and unforgettable storylines. I always tell anybody who critiques my work, blame Vince McMahon Sr.: that's who I grew up on and was educated by.

When I went to WCW and got a PhD in what REAL wrestling politics looked like, I guess you would say that's when the bloom was off the rose—an expression VKM used all the time. It was during that time that my pure, innocent love of the business started to wane. When I went home from WCW in January of 2000 and returned three months later, I returned to a *job* . . . no longer a love.

I think it was when I became an on-air character that everything started to change. Prior, I was just a writer/producer by the name of Vince Russo, who led the charge of the WWF as they brought the wrestling product into the 21st century through a lengthy and successful run called the Attitude Era. I was nameless and faceless during that surge that turned into a historic time in the business. When I made the decision to become a character on television—that's when things drastically changed.

As I've stated many times before, I made the decision to become an on-air character at WCW when the higher-ups started to put a ridiculous amount of pressure on me to raise the ratings over an unrealistic time period. What I told them was going to take months . . . they wanted in weeks. Their unrealistic, wishful thinking was exactly that: wishful. Their demands drove me to the attitude of, "Fine—if you want me to do it . . . I'll do it myself." That was a mistake that I regret to this day. The ramifications of my success as a character were something I could never have imagined.

My motivation was simple; if I was going to play the role of a brash, arrogant, conceited, stuck-up New Yawker, then I was going to magnify my personality a thousand times over. I was going to present Vince Russo—the character—as not only what everybody thought a New Yawker represented, but what everybody wanted a New Yawker to be.

You always hear about racism in wrestling, which I know didn't exist in the WWF—if Vince McMahon could make money with you, he didn't care if you were black, brown, yellow, white, OR GREEN. Sexism, on the other, hand *did* exist. When I was at the WWF, it was the good ol' boys' network, and if they felt a female was taking their spot, they got in Vince's ear and ended that female's run. I witnessed that with my own eyes. However, the one constant you never hear about are groups of people being stereotyped, being connected to a bias or prejudice. As a New Yawker, that was how I was perceived from day one among some in the wrestling business. Jim Cornette is your perfect example. Many "workers" in the business had their roots in the South, and they just despised anyone who represented the east coast. That dislike is magnified 10-fold when it comes to the Southern fan base.

So in an attempt for Vince Russo "the character" to be hated, I was going to be everything they wanted me to be. I first started seeing my public persona change with the dirt sheet writers. All of a sudden when they "heard" me and "saw" me, it was a much different narrative from when I was anonymously writing with Vince. Now, I was a typical loudmouth asshole New Yawker. That's when I first saw the hate come barreling in.

Honestly, I never gave a shit what the dirt writers thought, and I still don't. I know that those groups of people were about as jealous and envious as they come. They literally would have committed murder to be in my spot. Nothing has changed about that today. All of them are doing what they're doing because they simply will never get their dream job working for the WWE—and they know it.

Unfortunately, once social media started, that hatred grew exponentially. Now, it wasn't just a handful of fans—it was thousands who were spewing their disdain towards me and my work publicly, and on an hourly bias. Whether they were marks, subscribers to the dirt sheets, the "Cult of Cornette," whatever—there was a shitload of them. The reality is that supporters of mine aren't on wrestling's social media sites; believe it or not, they have real jobs and real lives. So the ratio of cons versus pros was about a thousand to one.

Today's wrestling marks are a hundred-percent responsible for my ill feelings towards the current wrestling business—hundred. percent. Yeah, wrestling isn't wrestling anymore, and great characters and compelling storylines have been replaced with the emphasis being on "the match," which now consists of acrobatic dance routines where you believe nothing is real because nobody sells anything. Yeah, that turned me off of the business, but it didn't make me *hate* it. No . . . it's today's fans that have transitioned my discontent to absolute hatred.

If I'm going to be blunt—yeah—today's marks make me sick. They're vile, hateful, disgusting, mean-spirited, vulgar, crass, and they don't give a shit as it relates to what they say about anybody, punching a keyboard from behind their computer/cell phone screen. They simply can't wait for their words of absolute hatred to come up before their eyes. It's almost as if they get off on their own hate speech.

And I say that with absolute certainty. It's not the business, nor the people in it. I experienced that for over two decades—it was the nature of the beast, and I just got used to it. There will always be politics in wrestling; there will always be bad people, that's just part of the very fiber of what the industry is and the people who are drawn to it. And that's in any and every business, so, yeah, it's just part of the Corporate World.

But, today's hardcore fan base? Just despicable people that I don't want to have anything to do with. And, man, make no mistake: the business itself has cultivated these vultures by catering to them—something I thought I'd never see in my lifetime. In 30 years, the WWE went from VKM's inner circle getting a good chuckle out of Meltzer's dirt sheet in the morning to now actually catering to that same audience he represents. They dictate to the WWE, tell them what they want to see and what they don't, and the WWE follows their every command. They have power now, while the base of Casual Fans—the masses—has since moved on.

I always hear from these same marks how bitter I am, how irrelevant I am, how upset I am because the WWE and AEW won't "hire me." Yet another f-bomb coming—are you fucking kidding me? I'm not bitter at all; I absolutely love my life and would never trade what I'm doing now for anything. If I do come across as being "bitter"—because I don't have many nice things to say about the creative part of pro wrestling these days—it's because I feel they are phoning it in, and to me the casual wrestling fans deserve better—much better. If you are going to ask a casual to spend three hours of their Monday night with you, then at least try to entertain them. Don't give me a rinse-and-repeat television house show every Monday that is predictable and boring. They deserve better—try harder.

But, for the reasons I stated earlier, the WWE has become very complacent with the money they're raking in, due to the total incompetence of third parties signing them to huge deals but not knowing what they're actually getting. Don't believe me, then just ask FOX.

Yes, I feel bad that today I am an outsider—I feel like an outsider, and I don't belong. I am just not one of these guys that love the business I was in and would do anything possible to get the opportunity to re-enter it. I'm at the complete opposite end of that spectrum. But it does bother me that some of my peers, probably many of my peers, see me as "anti-wrestling," because I'm not. I'm just anti the *presentation* of today's wrestling, what it has become, and the savage cult of misfits sitting in the stands who changed it.

Man, I can't get any blunter than that.

62 A MAN NAMED JED

Throughout my entire lifetime, I have never been able to be complacent or just plain satisfied. I don't know what it is about me, but I get bored real easily. No matter how much older I get, I just can't relax, take a moment, settle in, stop and smell that basil. It's just not in my DNA, not in my makeup. I always need change . . . constant change. I don't like to stay at jobs long, I don't like to have the same schedule or routine for an extended period of time, I don't like to sit or stay in one place.

You have no idea how many times I've moved since I graduated college—let me take a moment to figure that out because it's way too many times to have a number off the top of my head . . . OK, I did the math—not including temporary housing, I moved eight times in the last 41 years. And that's exactly right—I get the itch to move about every five years. You have no idea what I've dragged Amy through during that time. Packing, moving, unpacking, always knowing that the stop was going to be temporary till Vince had to up and go . . . again.

Which leads me to my move to Evansville, Indiana. Yes, this was strange and bizarre even to me! For starters, as much as Evansville was an extremely important part of my life—being where I received my college education, adopted my work ethic, obtained lifelong friends, met, dated, and got engaged to my wife, for God's sake—I always labeled Evansville as a terrific *temporary* place to live. Unless you were born and raised there and that's all you know—no way, no how, should you permanently plant yourself there.

I've said over and over, I didn't mind living in the Midwest, and I really found the people to be genuinely hospitable and kind, but the hard facts were—unless you were attending college and perhaps in a frat, there is just nothing to do . . . literally. It's like you step outside your door, and there's no place to go. Much unlike Colorado, where you point yourself in any direction, travel 30 minutes, and you are in an absolute wonderland! BUT, that was almost 35 years ago . . . maybe the place has changed.

So, in 2017 we packed up and moved again, leaving beautiful Colorado for Amy's hometown of Evansville, Indiana . . . hoping for the best.

Yeah, you're right—What's !@#$%^& wrong with me?! What was going through my !@#$%^& head? Well, I'm not going to sit here and absolutely pummel the hell out of myself . . . there was a reason.

I don't know if it's because being a New Yawker through and through there are just some curiosities deep within my cerebrum that tend to make me want to go in a completely different direction. I have no idea, but anyway, a part of me has always had an infatuation with wanting to live in a log cabin. Weird, right? But it's there.

So, one day out of the blue, Amy shows me a log cabin in—where else—Evansville. Now, for starters, when I look at anything, the first thing I look at is the price. I believe this cabin was somewhere in the 250K range, so—check that box. From there, what's the acreage? What does the land look like? Well, in this case it was about four acres, with its own lake right in the backyard—check box number two. Third box: Was this a real log cabin? Many cabins have the outside esthetics of a real log cabin, but once you go inside—there are no freakin' logs. This one had logs. This was a real, authentic, hundred-percent bona fide log cabin.

With Amy's cousin a real estate agent in Evansville, I suggested to her that she ask Connie to just give us a virtual tour of the place—that's all it was going to be. So, Connie took her phone to the log cabin and walked us through it. I was intrigued. Well, perhaps more than intrigued as I suggested to Amy that we actually take a ride to Evansville and see it. If I'm going that far . . . yeah . . . I'm genuinely interested. Almost needless to say, we went to Evansville, and we both fell in love with the cabin.

So this is what I'm thinking, for shits and giggles let's just put our Broomfield, Colorado, house up for sale and see what happens. We figure that in the time it would take to get a bite on our house, the cabin would be long gone. But we put the house up for sale with our real estate agent, Alyssa—who is a freakin' shark. Alyssa is almost like family being how many houses we've bought and sold through her over the years.

Yeah—I should have known better. Not only did Alyssa get a bite the first day, but the offer was for more money than we were asking!

Was this . . . A SIGN?!

STREAM OF CONSCIOUSNESS

SIGNS

Are you one of those people who, when you are on the fence about something and you can't make a decision, is constantly looking for a sign? But, the only sign you are really interested in receiving is that sign that reads the way you want it to read?! We all do that—no doubt. I mean, have you ever received a sign that went the opposite way from the answer you were seeking? And, if so, have you disregarded that sign and looked for another sign with the right answer?!

I think the sign thing is all bullshit, a gimmick, unless it comes directly from God like the two crisp $50 bills in my pack of Doublemint. That was a REAL sign; it was divine and not man-made.

So, was this a sign? Alyssa listed our house and got an offer the next day for more than the asking price? Were Amy and I being "called" to pick up and move to our dream log cabin, on four acres, with a lake . . . in Evansville, Indiana? I wanted to take it as a sign so we "loaded up the truck and we moved to Evans-v" (sing that to the tune of *The Beverly Hillbillies* theme song).

Once we arrived, seeing the cabin was everything we thought it'd be. It was set back in the woods off a long dirt driveway. The scenery was off a postcard. We owned a yard far too big to even walk. And the lake? Stocked with catfish, even some albino ones. Man, this was as peaceful as peaceful can be. So quiet, still, serene, I felt like this was the payoff for my putting up with all the wrestling bullshit for all those years.

I loved this place; this is what I always wanted. And, hell yeah, I deserved it.

NOTE: I'll never forget, when we moved into our dream cabin, "Hillbilly" Jim Cornette told his "Cult" on his podcast that my wife and I had to go back to Evansville to move in with my in-laws because I was broke. What a !@#$%^& schmuck.

Man, I took such pride in this place. I single-handedly finished the entire basement, laying a wooden floor myself. I had a safe pool dye added to the lake to make it look like a blue oasis. I was able to obtain a $15,000 hot tub (that fit a small army) for $100 (they even delivered it) simply because somebody "wanted to get rid of it"—only in Evansville. Bumper pool, a cool set-up for all my vinyl . . . ahhh . . . deep, deep exhale. Perhaps the coolest perk was walking down to the water and hand-feeding the catfish every day. I swear, they would hear my footsteps and swim right up to me, knowing it was feeding time.

Man, it couldn't be THIS GOOD . . . could it?

No . . . it couldn't.

Nothing is perfect, and I understand that. So, there were some things Amy and I were going to have to live with. For starters, I had to mow the four acres, and you know how much I hate yard work. I was Eddie Albert on *Green Acres*. I can't tell you how many times I almost rolled our riding mower and chopped myself to pieces. We couldn't take a bath in the upstairs bathroom because every time you put the water on it would stream, not leak, *stream*, downstairs to the kitchen below. And lastly—believe it or not—there was no Internet. However, those were all issues that could be dealt with—the cabin itself was our sanctuary . . . for the time being, anyway.

Despite these "small" issues, there was one problem that couldn't be fixed. Whenever we decided to leave our cozy and comfortable nest . . . there was nowhere to go! Yeah—even though it was 35 years later . . . it was still bum-f*** Evansville, Indiana! There is nothing to do in that town—zero, zilch, donut, goose egg. A person can only go to Coconuts (an old-school record shop) and look at albums so many times. I was starting to get bored out of my mind . . . and fast. Amy had taken a job with the local school district, and I was spending a ton of my time in the cabin alone. After a while, not even the catfish were making me smile. But I know I've got to suck it up . . . I can't let Amy know how I'm feeling. So, I bit my tongue, and upper and lower lips, until a much bigger issue arose.

63 "HILLBILLY" JIM, KENNY BOLIN, AND THE RESTRAINING ORDER

Man, that could be the name of a blockbuster movie.

Yeah, you've all heard about the restraining order against Hillbilly Jim, but you haven't a clue how it came about. Some even claim I was "afraid" of Jim—yeah—he's going to beat me over the head with an '80's tennis racket, the one with the fuzzy cover maybe.

Here's how it all started.

My mother recently had passed. Jim being the absolute assclown that he is actually goes on his podcast and makes a joke out of it. I didn't hear the show, but I got a call from my pizon, Vito LoGrasso, aka Big Vito, saying, "Vin . . . you gonna let him slide on that? It's your matha—you've got to say somethin."

So I did.

However, rather than stoop to Jim's childish, third-grade, lowest level by assaulting him with names, I cut a YouTube video, sarcastically "apologizing" to him for Vince McMahon choosing me over him, Dixie choosing me over him, and for him breaking both his knees falling off a scaffold—because he didn't know how to take a bump—which I think was the one that really got him.

Jim went NUCLEAR on me on his next show—I had beaten him at his own game, and he couldn't handle it.

That right there should be the end of the story because Jim has made a career out of burying and insulting me for the past 25 years. It was just business as usual—it's his routine, his shtick. But here's where the story takes an odd twist.

It was around this time that I received an email from an extremely "unusual suspect," his name . . . Kenny Bolin. When I first heard from Kenny, I really had no idea who he was. However, what immediately caught my eye was that he was a character through and through, and you know I love characters. Through Twitter, Kenny reached out to me and asked me to be a guest on his show. He told me that he'd been best friends with Cornette since childhood . . .

Wait a minute. Kenny . . . ? Kenny . . . I've heard that before as it pertains to Hillbilly Jim. Kenny . . . no, can't be . . . cannot be!

That name, Kenny . . . I just kept hearing it over and over in my head. Where do I know that name? Then it hits me, going back to my WWF days, when doing their best Jim Cornette impression, JR and Bruce always used to refer to a Kenny while putting on a *very* high-pitched voice.

"Oh my God . . . Kenny," they would always say.

They were referring to KENNY BOLIN. I had no idea at the time, but now I understood. Kenny, through JR and Bruce, had become infamous to me, even though who he was was always a mystery—that mystery was now solved.

So now it all registers. Kenny (in a high-pitched voice) is going to bring me on his show in an attempt to humiliate and embarrass me? Come on, man, how gullible do you think I am? Well, very I guess, because at that point Kenny began selling me the car, the warranty, the undercoat protection, the whole shebang, swearing to me that he wouldn't go down that road. I learned in a hurry—you just can't say no to Kenny Bolin. Kenny's that girlfriend—she might be OK, not hot, but OK for the time being; I know I could do better. Meanwhile, she persists for days, months, weeks, and now you have a marriage certificate, a mortgage, three kids, and a St. Bernard with her!

But, man, I'm the guy with a big mouth who always claims to not run from anybody. So, what the hell—I'll go on with the "King" (his self-proclaimed moniker). I did—and you won't believe what happened next.

I have no problem saying this—I became an instant mark for "The King" Kenny Bolin.

For years, I have pointed out Dutch Mantel and Jim Cornette as being the two most quick-witted individuals I've ever met. They are just so sharp; their minds almost work like computers. The second after a sentence comes out of your mouth, they fire back with comments that only they can muster. And I'm not talking about clichés or coined phrases, I'm talking about a use of the human language in a way which you have never witnessed before.

For example: "He's deader than Kelsey's Nuts." That was one of my favorite ones—to this day, I have no idea what it means, but to Jim and Dutch it definitely means something important.

Within the first five minutes, I was hooked on Kenny (said in a high-pitched voice). Man, the dude was just so smart, clever, funny, interesting, unique, and, of course, a one-of-a-kind character. Kenny went about his line of questioning when it came to my relationship with his childhood friend, and he listened. For the first time in about 20 years, he was now hearing the other side of the story.

After our conversation, Kenny realized that I wasn't the "shit-stain New Yawker" he had been hearing about for two decades, and I don't know about hell freezing over—but the King and I became friends. I told you, I love characters, and KB wrote the handbook on "How to be a living, breathing, entertaining character."

What happened next didn't surprise me. After a 50-year friendship, Jim Cornette cut off Kenny Bolin and ended their relationship because Kenny had me on his show. This is typical Jim Cornette. This would be the equivalent of me cutting off Disco if he did Eric Bischoff's *83 Weeks*. But that's Jim. I mean what was really going through his mind? That Kenny was disloyal to him because he had a conversation with me? No, the reality was that Jim had to keep the "Vince Russo storyline" alive with his "cult," so he had no choice other than to end a five-decade relationship.

But . . . I'm the shit stain.

OK, so here is where the plot thickens. Remember, this is coming off the heels of my sarcastic apology video, so Jim is already HOT to begin with.

After Kenny and I did his show, I get a phone call from Kenny. He basically says, "Vince, now that I know who you are . . . I've got to tell you something."

Kenny paused, then he went on. "Vince, I feel I have to tell you this after our conversation." Another pause. "Before you and I did that show, I went out to lunch with Jimmy . . ." Then he proceeded to tell me something I was not prepared to hear.

It's been a long time, so I'm paraphrasing here, but the two most important things that Kenny said were:

1. He's going to send people after you.
2. File a restraining order immediately.

64 SHOTGUN ANNIE

When you look at Kenny's warning, that immediately erases any suggestion that I was actually afraid of Jim Cornette, as some of my adversaries would have wanted you to believe. Cornette was never the threat, but indeed his cult of followers was. I mean, have you ever read the comments from some of these whack-jobs? Have you ever seen what they look like? A lot of these people are "backwards," and that's about as polite as I can be. They are capable of anything, and that's why I took Kenny's warning seriously.

Now, remember, I lived in a log cabin in the woods and off a dirt road. Could you image one of these yahoos driving out in their pickup and confronting Amy home alone? That's what I was taking quite seriously. However, I didn't file for the restraining order immediately. The first step was to try and handle the situation myself.

So, the first thing I did was phone my brother-in-law, Jeff, who is, let's say, a gun enthusiast. As in, a week earlier, I had gone to a sporting goods store with Jeff, and he was literally packing heat. I explained my situation, and he came to the cabin later that day.

Now, you have to envision this, because it really took place. Right there in my gravel driveway, Jeff attempted to teach me how to cock, lock, and load a SHOTGUN. It was the first and only time I ever held a gun in my hands. As I'm standing there listening to Jeff's instructions, I'm thinking to myself—so what—some !@#$%^& Jim Cornette loon is going to pull up in my driveway in a beat-up old pickup and what . . . I'm gonna blow his !@#$%^& brains out?!

When I realized what I was doing, thank God the rational side of my brain kicked in. It was then that I decided to do things rationally and leave a trail, God forbid something did happen. Remember, this is the guy that told Terry Taylor when he was let go from TNA that if he could kill Vince Russo and get away with it . . . he'd do it in a heartbeat. I'm going to take that seriously, especially now when I was literally living just a car ride away from Cornette Country.

NOTE: Terry Taylor informed the TNA lawyers about Jim's comment. The legal team took it as a terroristic threat. They called me with a plan to have Dixie schedule a meeting with Jim to discuss "future TNA business" in order to have him arrested and taken into custody upon his arrival. I thanked them for looking out for me and attempting to protect me, but I told them it wasn't necessary. Hindsight being 20/20 . . . maybe it was.

So, I went to the county courthouse, told my story to a judge, and he issued the restraining order. Of course, Jim treated this as a joke, going so far as to autograph the restraining order and offer it for sale to those in his cult who apparently couldn't find better ways to spend their money. Again, at that point I could easily have gone back to the judge to report Cornette for doing this, but I didn't; my intent was just to leave a legal trail, God forbid something did happen.

65 ON THE ROAD AGAIN

At this point, our dream cabin on a lake in the woods was quickly turning into a huge regret. I was even in danger of losing my ability to broadcast because we were in such a rural area that there was no Wi-Fi. I literally had to get a ginormous satellite dish installed on top of the cabin, which gave me the ability to record via a shitty connection where the audio and video quality of my show wasn't worth the price of subscribing. Man, all of this was a hot mess, and we were only about six months in. Every day, I would just sit on my La-Z-Boy, staring at the TV, not knowing what the !@#$%^& to do.

I was quickly reaching that level of depression that I had experienced when I moved to Atlanta to work for WCW. That was perhaps the lowest point in my life, all of it documented in my second book, *Rope Opera: How WCW Killed Vince Russo*. Man, I couldn't let Amy know how I was feeling. After all these years, she was finally back home with her three sisters and her mother. This was all familiar to her—she was comfortable there.

Or . . . so I thought.

One day, Amy came home from work and she said, "Vin . . . I can't do this anymore. We've got to get out of here. I'm going crazy!" As they say in the Midwest—I about shit my britches! Amy had been feeling the exact same way I was, but she was just as afraid to say anything to me as I was to her. Man, thank God we were on the same page. After only eight months of living in that cabin, we packed up and headed back to Colorado.

66 BACK HOME AGAIN/MICKIE JAMES/ROCKY MOUNTAIN PRO

In one of my favorite John Denver songs, "Back Home Again," substitute "the mountains" in for "this old farm," and you get that "long-lost friend" I'd been missing. Looking back, I have no idea why I ever left Colorado. I love it here, it's just home . . . it's just me. There is such a sense of peace and tranquility when I get in my Jeep Wrangler, roof down, and drive anywhere, feeling the beauty, power, grace, and majesty of the Rocky Mountains. And, yes, they are purple!

So being back in the place I should have never left, it was time to get back to work again, full throttle, with Wi-Fi that actually functioned. Doing my podcast, I was always busy, always doing something, never looking to add more . . . but "more" always seems to add itself.

Man, I just checked back through my emails . . . it's hard to fathom that I met Matt Yaden eight years ago. We're coming on a decade, and it seems like it's only been a few months. Matt was the owner and proprietor of a wrestling school and a small indy promotion in Colorado. Honestly, I can't even remember what he first called his company—the original name sucked—I think it was NRW, and I couldn't even tell you what that stood for, except maybe the last letter was Wrestling. Eventually, I would suggest a new name for Matt's promotion, which he soon adopted, and thus Rocky Mountain Pro was born. God, I still love that name. And I didn't even trademark it or charge Matt a dime . . . is it too late?

I met Matt through the great Nick Aldis, the current acting GM of WWE *SmackDown*, and I'm going to say this simply to piss him off and because I love her—Nick is also the husband of perhaps the nicest person in the world . . . Mickie James. So yeah, he's MR. MICKIE JAMES!

Let me tell you why Mickie will always and forever have a special place in my heart. It goes back to before Nick signed with the WWE, where he was promoting some of his own shows and events. One of those was "The Trial of Vince Russo," that was going to be presented across the pond. The show was a gimmick, based around the ups and downs of my career. You see—I can take a joke. After Nick laid it out as being a show based on comedy and satire, I took the job.

Now, if you know me, you know I absolutely hate flying. The reasons for this loathing are numerous: Your plane can crash, burn, explode, and you will be killed well before contact. Plus, the hundreds and hundreds of flights I had already been on while in the wrestling business had taken their toll on me. And these flights to England are hours long, and I have issues with staying in a restricted space for a very long time . . . But this was for Nick and Mickie, so I was going to suck it up.

STREAM OF CONSCIOUSNESS

"Suck It Up" has been my mantra throughout my entire life. Don't bitch, complain, kvetch, or bellyache when you have to do something you don't want to do. Just suck it up and do it. That's it. No hemming and hawing, just !@#$%^& suck it up.

Today, for instance, I have to go to Rocky Mountain Pro. I have to shoot dozens of pre-tapes in a very limited amount of time. I will be working a nonstop day, on my feet for a solid 10 hours. You think I want to do that at my age? No, I don't—so, this morning I'm getting into "suck it up" mode. Just shut your !@#$%^& mouth, put on your big boy pants, strap up those boots, get out there, and *suck it up*.

My flight to England would have a stop at JFK in New York. I was thankful for that because at the time, my mother, who was battling dementia, was not faring very well. This gave me an opportunity to check in with my dad between flights. But when I called my father, I could tell by the tone of his voice that my mom was fading. My dad is always upbeat and jovial, but this time he just wasn't himself.

I've got to tell you, my father has had a difficult time conveying his feelings for as far back as I can remember. He just doesn't talk about things that are personal, and he never has. I honestly believe I have picked up that trait from him. I don't like dealing with my feelings. That's why writing this book is almost a vital exercise for me. Through my keyboard, feelings have just flowed from the first sentence I typed. Emotions just started pouring out—all over the place. And I can't edit anything out, I can't. Everything you have read this far has been needed to be said, if not for anything but my own mental and emotional wellness.

My dad would have never asked me to fly to Ocala, he just wouldn't, but it was plainly clear that I had to. This could be the last time I would get to see my mom. So, badly shaken, I hung up with my father, and I knew that I had to call Nick to let him know that my connecting flight was going to be to Florida and not the UK. When I called . . . Mickie answered. For some reason, as soon as I heard her voice I just started sobbing.

NOTE: Once again *admitting* I was CRYING.

I told Mickie of my call with my dad; I told her that I thought my mom was dying. Now understand, she and Nick had a shitload of money tied up in this venture, and it all revolved around me. I'm literally giving her a day's notice to come up with a plan B—if that were even possible. Man, at that point, I saw the real Mickie James, not the WWE superstar that we've all grown to know and love, but the woman, the wife . . . the mother. Mickie could not have been more compassionate, sympathetic, and understanding. She told me that I shouldn't waste one second, I needed to get to my mom as quickly as possible. She never once brought up the show or the severe headaches this could cause her and Nick. At that moment, all she cared about was what I was experiencing.

I've never forgotten that, and I never will. To this moment, I know that Mickie has no clue the impact her words had on my heart. You just don't experience that often in wrestling, a business in which, no matter what your circumstances, the show must always come first.

Man, that was a long roundabout to bring me back to Matt Yaden.

STREAM OF CONSCIOUSNESS

The only time I had heard the term "roundabout" was back in 1971, when the progressive rock band Yes released it as a single.

That song is on my top 21 songs to play when I kick the bucket, along with these favorites:

"Rocky Mountain High"—John Denver
"Day Tripper"—The Beatles
"Stay (I Missed You)"—Lisa Loeb
"Me and Bobby McGee"—Janis Joplin
"Maybe I'm Amazed"—Paul McCartney
"What's Up (What's Goin' On)"—4 Non Blondes
"Stiff Upper Lip"—AC/DC
"Midnight Train to Georgia"—Gladys Knight & the Pips
"Crumblin' Down"—John Mellencamp
"Gimme Shelter"—The Rolling Stones
"New York's Not My Home"—Jim Croce
"Ball of Confusion (That's What the World Is Today)"—The Temptations
"Death on Two Legs"—Queen
"That's Life"—Frank Sinatra
"Seven Nation Army"—The White Stripes
"Zanzibar"—Billy Joel
"Fire and Ice"—Pat Benatar
"Wait Your Turn"—Rihanna
"Charisma"—KISS
"I Hate Myself for Loving You"—Joan Jett and the Blackhearts

But getting back to the roundabout, no, I never had to drive by way of one until we moved to Colorado. If you don't know what a roundabout is, it's like you drive around a circle with three or four different ways out. However, there are also three or four ways coming in, so it's all about timing. We have a roundabout about three miles from my house. My wife curses it every time she has to drive it, and it drives me insane.

There are other things my wife does behind the wheel of a car that have worn on me over our 42 years of marriage. For starters, she has such a heavy brake foot. Every time she hits the brake, it's at the last moment and with all she's got. In other words—my head snaps forward causing whiplash at every stop sign and red light. Also, when my wife has to merge into oncoming traffic, she looks both ways and says, every !@#$%^& time, "I can't see." . . . Every time. Now, if you are saying that you can't see, how do you think you are making the person in the passenger seat—ME—feel?! It drives me !@#$%^& nuts!

Back to Matt Yaden.

Nick and Mickie were in town to work an indy show with a promoter by the name of Matt Yaden. Over dinner—that I paid for—Nick put over Matt and said I should hook up with him, suggesting maybe we could work together. So I did exactly that. Upon my first meeting with Matt, I could tell almost immediately that he was too nice a guy to be in the wrestling business. Matt wasn't your typical "snake in the grass" promoter, he was a regular guy, single dad, just trying to make a living doing something he loved.

Matt explained to me that sometime earlier he moved to Nashville for a year to work in the office at TNA, looking for an opportunity. Keep in mind . . . he had to move away from his daughter for this. Of course, being wrestling, those promises were never fulfilled, so Matt was back in the Rockies making a go of it on his own.

After hitting it off, Matt and I came to an agreement that I would write and produce his wrestling shows, while also going down to his school a couple of times a week to help out with the students. Man, there was a lot of really good young, raw, unknown talent there, and I was excited for the opportunity.

Unfortunately, it wasn't long before I started seeing a trend continue that I first experienced at TNA nearly 20 years ago. The younger generation, who are 30 years my junior and have done absolutely nothing in the business—let alone in their lives—seem to know more about the ins and outs of professional wrestling than I—a guy who's worked in the industry for over two decades—ever will. Now, guys, chalk it up to the "proud Italian" in me, or whatever, but one thing a person should never do is disrespect me. I'm not going to take that from anybody, let alone some 20-something, know-nothing "children."

When the situation arose, I tried to handle it the right way, by attempting to have a grown-up conversation, but that didn't work. Once I was cussed out over the phone by somebody half my age—I told Matt I was done with Rocky Mountain Pro.

So I left.

But, man, I get attached to people . . . good people . . . because there aren't really too many out there. So Matt and I kept in touch frequently over the years, only to try it again . . . with the same results. The second go-round, the players changed, but the disrespect remained . . . so I left a second time.

Currently, Matt and I are trying to get our marriage back together for the third time. What's ironic is that, through it all, the issues have never been between him and me. There is a respect, admiration, and friendship there, but, when you mix that with pro wrestlers—to make matters worse, these are "wannabe" pro wrestlers—it's hard to stay married.

Matt Yaden is one of those guys who is just too good and too nice for the wrestling business. It's just not in Matt's makeup to be a shark. But, for all his dreams and all his ambitions revolving around the wrestling business, he is in the best spot possible—working for himself, a hundred-percent in control of his failures and successes.

UPDATE: As I'm copyediting this book, the third time with Matt and Rocky Mountain Pro did indeed happen . . . only for it to end again. But this time it was more related to finances than disrespect.

67 CHANNEL ATTITUDE/ BRAND MEMBERS TURN

With all the money that was both spent and wasted in developing the new site once RELM was dissolved, my vision was to build a podcasting platform that would house dozens of shows, covering dozens of topics. I was looking to start my own network, as Dusty would say, "if you will." So I came up with the name Channel Attitude, which was perfect for me. I trademarked it, had the site designed—finally—and went into business.

First thing on my agenda was to find talented podcasters—entertainers, not talking heads—who were passionate about their field of expertise. As I mulled over various names, I get a call from Jeff Lane, who suggested former MLB World Series champion Aubrey Huff. Now, a few months earlier I did a show with Aubrey as my guest, and the two of us had a great chemistry. At this point in his career, even though Aubrey had long since retired, he'd become a red-hot button on social media, being an opinionated, outspoken right-winger. Aubrey was very much into America and being a man's-man, and he strongly supported the right to bear arms and . . . Donald Trump.

At the time, I thought this was a brilliant idea from Jeff—man, we needed that first host to be loud and controversial in order to put young Channel Attitude on the map. So, I figured, what the heck—let me give Mr. Huff a call. So I did—and he AGREED! I never expected that to be so easy. Now that Aubrey was on board, I wanted to make sure that we had somebody on the left to balance things out. That was the original vision for Channel Attitude: to not only have something for everybody, but to hopefully have a forum where both sides actually communicate and talk.

With that plan, the first person that came to mind was my good friend, someone I respect more than just about anybody in the wrestling business, Kevin Nash. Kevin is what they call a "lefty," and having both him and Aubrey on the same network would have been bananas. So I called Kevin and presented the idea to him, and he seemed to be interested. After that conversation, I then contacted Aubrey with the idea of possibly bringing him and Kevin together, and he was very much open to it as well.

Man, this would have been ideal. Getting Aubrey Huff and Kevin Nash together on a podcast, two brilliant minds with two extremely different viewpoints—that is exactly how I had envisioned Channel Attitude. Unfortunately, in life, things don't always turn out the way we plan. The idea was to get Aubrey up and running first, which included schooling him a bit on podcasting and setting him up from a technical standpoint, being he was new to this forum. Once that was in place, I would go forward with my conversation with Kevin.

Off the Cuff with Aubrey Huff kicked off sometime around August 2021. On his podcast, Aubrey held nothing back; he had very much the same presence he created on social media, a presence I might add that had literally gotten him blackballed from the San Francisco Giants and any 2010 or 2012 World Series celebrations that the team would hold. And Aubrey was a huge part of that first World Series win, the first championship in 56 years for the Giants. However, that didn't faze Aubrey, who made it clear to me that he just didn't give a !@#$%^& about what others thought about his opinion. Again, this was the man who once said to me, "Vince—I have f***-you money." So there's that.

Call me naive, stupid, imbecilic, whatever you would like, but I swear to you . . . what happened next, I never saw coming.

After Aubrey dropped his first show, a handful of Brand members, well, two, if you want me to be exact, started going on social media, publicly stating how "disappointed" they were in me. How could I allow Aubrey Huff, with his beliefs and thoughts, to have a show on my network? Well, to me that answer was simple: I am an advocate of freedom of speech. And

I believe we are all entitled to that, whether we agree or don't. To me, that's what being an American citizen is all about.

With those comments, I again made it clear that Channel Attitude was going to be a forum for all voices—that's what I believed in. Aubrey's show just happened to come first based on Jeff's suggestion—that's all. As I stated earlier, once his show was up and running the plan was to get Kevin aboard. I had every intention of making that happen.

But I was never allowed to get to that point. The two, who were once extremely loyal to me and RussosBrand, went all out on a public hate campaign against me. Here we go again with that cancel culture bullshit. They got ugly, and they got ugly fast. I never expected this; I never even considered it, to be honest with you.

STREAM OF CONSCIOUSNESS

This is why I hate politics and everything concerning politics.

Look, I have stated loud and clear to my audience from day one—the way I was raised: I was taught to respect the seat and whoever's in it. Republican, Democrat, it didn't matter—we the people voted the president in, and we need to respect the seat. Hell, the bible even tells you that.

I never talk politics on my show, never have, and I would never so much as dare to tell you who to vote for. That is your decision, not mine. If I am trying to force my vote upon you, I am basically telling you you are an idiot, without a mind of your own, therefore I have to tell you who to vote for. I don't disrespect anybody in that matter. I believe truly and deeply that we were all created equal, and we were all created with brains to think for ourselves. You will never know who I'm voting for, and I would never impose my will on anybody.

So, it was another "smear Vince campaign," and I'd lost count at that point how many times I'd now experienced that. Bottom line, I guess they win and I lose . . . it wasn't worth the time or aggravation. Aubrey himself got worn out over the backlash of just his opinion; and, that's all it was—an opinion. After only a few shows, he ended his podcast. And the money I invested, not to mention the vision I had for Channel Attitude, came to a halt. To this day, it hasn't recovered; somebody is always going to be offended, somebody is always going to be upset, mad, infuriated, and as they say—you can't please everybody. But with social media—attempting to manage that becomes a full-time job and an absolute waste of your time and energy, so you just move on . . . and that's what I did.

UPDATE: As of the editing of this book, one of the Brand turncoats has apologized for their actions through email. I was very happy to welcome them back.

68 THANK GOD FOR TONY KHAN

While my master plan for Channel Attitude died before it could even breathe on its own, there is always something else that just seems to appear out of thin air that grabs your attention and redirects your focus. That's why I absolutely mean it when I say—thank God for Tony Khan!

A billionaire's kid who was booking wrestling shows out of his backpack when he was 10, Tony Khan's dream became a reality when he financially backed an idea by Cody Rhodes and the Young Bucks and gave birth to All Elite Wrestling. AEW started as just an arena show, but once Tony was reeled in, it became a full-fledged wrestling company with a television rights deal on TBS/TNT.

Now, understand, I had no idea who Tony Khan was, nor did anybody else for that matter, but he quickly gained my attention when in an effort to get over with the marks, he decided to comment on me, without ever knowing or even having a conversation with me. Basically what Tony Khan said was, Vince Russo went into WCW when it had a hangnail . . . and he proceeded to cut off the whole arm.

Interesting. This coming from a guy who never wrote, produced, formatted a single wrestling show? Never created a character, wrote dialogue, built storylines, or was ever even backstage at a show? Right from the jump, Tony told me he was nothing more than a wrestling mark. He would soon verify that by publicly pledging his lifelong, undying love of Dave Meltzer.

So, Tony started *AEW Dynamite* on TBS with his inaugural audience being 1.4 million people. Now, if you watched that first show, you knew there wasn't a snowman's chance in hell of him maintaining that number. Why? Simply because the show was intended—built and designed—for a very niche audience. The presentation consisted of wrestling match after wrestling match, with high spot atop high spot, no psychology, characters, or storylines in sight.

Yes—the show was nothing but a five-star Dave Meltzer jerk-off fest.

The casual wrestling fans, or television viewers, were not going to make this a part of their Wednesday night routine, simply because it was not the pro wrestling/sports entertainment they grew up on. This was Cirque du Soleil, a bunch of flip, flop, and flying that looked as fake as hell, as nobody sold anything and they all kicked out of everything. And the stars themselves—with the exception of a few, they all looked like that next-door neighbor you'd casually wave to when he's out there weeding the yard. They were nobodies who looked like nobodies, with no business being in a wrestling ring let alone on prime-time TV.

STREAM OF CONSCIOUSNESS

Ah . . . *the dream*: my favorite topic that comes out of the mouth of any so-called professional wrestler who really has no reason to be there.

"I had a dream this, I had a dream that, etc., etc., etc." You'd think they were Martin Luther King Jr. on the steps of the Lincoln Memorial.

"When I was eight years old and I watched *WrestleMania*, I had a dream of becoming yada, yada, yada."

Hate to break the news; you know why it was a dream? Because it was supposed to be just that—it was never supposed to happen—improbable, impossible, no way . . . no how. That's why you were dreaming about it.

I take great offense to the fact that today anybody can become a professional wrestler—anybody. It doesn't matter your size, your shape, your skill set, your ability to convince an audience that anything you are doing or saying is real, and forget about having the it factor . . . you certainly don't need that.

No other "sport" is like that—none. To play in the NFL, MLB, NHL, or NBA, you have to be special. You have to stand out. You have to be better than the rest. You have to be one of the selected few. Not in pro wrestling—all you need is a hope and a dream, and you are on your way.

The real question is, How the !@#$%^& are they getting through the system? How the !@#$%^& are they making it to the main stage? Are Triple H and Shawn Michaels really that bad judges of talent as the gatekeepers of NXT? How can they be? If anyone understands what it takes to make it in wrestling—it's them! So, what it is then? Some think that Triple H and Shawn are securing their place in history—their legendary status of being the best that ever did it—by only promoting those who don't have the tools or personality to ever reach that level. Can that be the case? Because, unless you are second generation, or put in nearly a decade in the indies, nobody who comes up from NXT ever makes it on the main stage—they all become just another name on the roster, a good lil' hand that will never get over. Now put your 50-50 booking into play, and you have a roster full of mediocrity.

And that's exactly what you have today.

DREAM, MY ASS!

But this is what the billionaire's kid wanted—he was booking for himself and not the masses. And, with hindsight being 20/20, I guess that's OK when money isn't a part of the equation. When it's not about business and it's just about playing with live-action wrestling figures, then what does it matter . . . ? It simply doesn't.

Fast-forward five years, and TK and AEW have succeeded in losing half of their audience. Now, where that might indeed seem bleak, there is in fact a silver lining—Tony Khan himself may well have become the greatest character in the history of the business.

Tony has become the go-to of RussosBrand. The dude has brought me and my viewers/listeners five years of pure entertainment and joy! He has made himself the face of his own company, putting himself out there in the spotlight well over any wrestler on the roster. He does every interview, addresses every tweet, and, oh, those scrums.

AEW has been stealing a page from the Japanese playbook, where it is customary for legendary wrestling companies, like New Japan Pro-Wrestling, to hold press conferences after their shows. The term generally used for these post-event gatherings is "scrums." Now, keep in mind, the basic concept as it pertains to these scrums is utterly, as Wade Keller would say, PREPOSTEROUS! You are attempting to hold a shoot, or REAL press conference based around a work, or FAKE business. The whole notion of the idea is utterly moronic.

But . . . not to Tony Khan.

The "daddy" of AEW embraced this concept as a wrestling mark, and now has adopted it after every major AEW Premium Live Event (PLE). So, after every show, he keeps the talent over at least an additional hour, or two, and holds a legit, real, worked, fake press conference.

Now, before we even get into that cluster, let's first address this. If you actually know and understand the "boys," then you are fully aware that once the show is over and the final bell has rung, they want to get the hell out of there! Their day probably started sometime at around 5 a.m. when they got up, threw down a quick breakfast, and proceeded to drive themselves to the airport. From there, it's finding a parking spot, going through security, hopping on a tram, getting to your gate and praying to God that your flight isn't delayed. Then, you board a plane and wait . . . then you take off. You then land . . . and wait again, until you can deplane. Once you finally arrive you go to baggage claim to retrieve all your wrestling shit, deal with people wanting autographs at 8 a.m., maybe grab a coffee, then either search for your ride, who of course is late, or wait on line at Hertz or whatever bargain rental car agency awaits you. I'm not even going to discuss the possibilities of the car you rented not being available . . . yet.

Now, you don't have time to head to your hotel to get settled. You schlep it all straight to the building so you are not late, and fined, then you sit around and wait all day for your marching orders to know what the hell you're doing. Once that happens, you now get together with whoever you're working with and go over your match for at least a couple of hours.

We haven't even gotten to the ring yet.

Then . . . you finally have your match. You hope and pray that you don't get hurt, because you're going to be doing this all over again . . . the very next week. You have your match, your body hurts—hell, everything hurts. All you want to do is take a shower, get back in your rental car, maybe stop and get a quick unhealthy bite to eat, and drive to your hotel and put your GD head on the pillow.

That's all you want. That's all you think about all day long.

But TK, TK doesn't understand all that, and he clearly doesn't respect the time of the talent. Because after everything I just described, TK drags these poor slobs out in front of a sea of wrestling marks who call themselves journalists, to play Wrestling Press Conference.

But there's more! I haven't even gotten to the best part . . .

So the marks ask their Wrestling Press Conference questions. Some are a shoot; some are going along with the act. Yes, it's bizarre, totally bizarre; however, the best part of this entire clusterf*** is that Tony, himself, is sitting front and center of this ridiculous catastrophe from beginning to end. Why . . . ? We still have no idea. But yeah, Tony is the focal point of his own mock press conference, overshadowing any wrestler who may be sitting next to him. And . . . all this is magical . . . totally magical: Our best content comes from these scrums. Regardless of how idiotic and insane they actually are, I for one hope they never go away.

69 CATERING TO THE MARKS

Tony Khan stealing a wrestling mark play from a wrestling mark playbook, in this case NJPW, doesn't surprise me at all. In fact, I wouldn't have expected anything less. Where the absolute shock came from was when Triple H and the WWE followed suit. Never in my wildest, sick and twisted imaginings, did I think I would ever see that. The only difference is that Trips doesn't sit in for the whole thing—he makes himself available only at either the beginning or the end to address the mark questions.

This is what is killing the business. You actually opened up your door and invited the wrestling marks to come inside, kick off their shoes, and be a part of the show. If you have a presence on social media, you are allowed in. It doesn't matter what your credentials are, or if you have any credibility at all, all that matters is that you have followers.

It's both a disgrace and an embarrassment to put the boys and girls through this torture—it shows zero respect or consideration for their time kowtowing to grown-ass adults in their thirties acting like they haven't even reached puberty yet playing "Never Have I Ever" with talent . . . I'm going to drop an f-bomb again: it's a fucking disgrace to the business and to everyone who was ever a part of it.

So now, the million-dollar question: WHY? Why would you allow them in our house when they've never been allowed in before? The answer is simple—in Tony's case, he's just a full-fledged mark himself, who needs the accolades and attention; but, Trips and the WWE are obviously using these lowly, unaccredited marks to promote and put them over. Think about it; are any of these Media Marks going to say anything negative about your company in fear of them maybe losing their press credentials? Are they? No, they're just going to stick their mark heads straight up your keister and tell their fan base on an ongoing loop how great you are.

But here's the ironic thing: Whether they were or were not invited to the scrum, wouldn't they do that anyway? We are talking about people with zero lives here. They eat, drink, piss, poop pro wrestling 24/7. Every second of every single day—that's all they do. There's nothing else in their lives. So, the bottom line is, good, bad, or indifferent—they're going to be talking about you anyway.

UPDATE: As of the editing of this book, the WWE has stopped doing after-event scrums. But—for good reason. When Brock Lesnar returned, WWE brass did not want to take any chances on one of these marks asking Brock about his involvement in the Janel Grant case. (You will be caught up on all that a few pages from now.)

Yes, the entire world of professional wrestling and those who run it are now catering to a fan base that they already have. There are no new fans being cultivated, they are just raping and gouging money from the sea of marks that live for that very existence. Am I being rude? Absolutely I am, but that's the way it is. The wrestling business has killed the wrestling business.

If you are a WWE fan, WWE can do nothing wrong and you hate AEW; if you are an AEW fan—the same the other way around. They're not fans anymore, they're a cult, and this has cast such a shadow of negativity upon the business; you are either on one side, or the other. Add to that, if you are a casual viewer who just wants to enjoy the show, you are not welcomed—you are not one of us—the fandom is ours exclusively and you are not allowed in. They've succeeded in running the REAL wrestling fans, what they would deem the "casuals," off.

Yeah, man, these lunatics now actually believe they are part of the show. Meanwhile, what they don't understand is that they are all controlled by the WWE. They are all programmed to spend all their money so they can have the privilege and honor of singing along to wrestlers' theme songs at the top of their lungs. We normal fans laugh at this—we laugh at them—and as far as we're concerned, you can have it.

My days of being a pro wrestling fan are over. To be fair, the death of that fandom probably happened some 25 years ago when I saw the paradigm switch starting to take over. I didn't—and still don't—want to be a part of this world, and I don't want to be associated with these people. Harsh, yes, but that's the way I feel.

70 MY LAST EXCHANGE WITH VINCE MCMAHON

I swear to you, it's not that I need the money, nor is it that I miss it, but sometimes when I watch the WWE I get so disgusted with their boring, passive, lackadaisical, "the money is already in the bank" booking, that I get the urge to reach out to them in an effort to just try to make the shows better. Now, understand I know how full-bore insane that is, but man, if I have to sit there and watch five hours of this shit every week . . . can we at least attempt to make it better?

There's always, "Vince—shouldn't you be giving back to the business rather than shitting on it?" Well, I guess you can say "maybe" . . . but, then again, this isn't the business that I was in. It's a completely different animal. So, I don't even know why I reached out. The idea of me working in that broken and flawed creative system is ludicrous. I would never last, not even for a day. And I'm not going on the road, I'm not setting one foot in an arena, so what am I doing? The simple answer is: I don't know—but I did it anyway.

So, a few years ago I reached out to Vince McMahon for the very last time. The product had reached rock bottom again, and I guess I just couldn't stand it anymore. I sent Vince an email and almost immediately I got a text on my phone from a Connecticut number. I immediately thought there's no way he's getting back to me this quickly, so I called my friend Bubba Ray Dudley to confirm the phone number—it was indeed Vince.

What follows is my last exchange of emails with Vince McMahon—I've never released them before, but I think you'll find them highly entertaining.

> From: vincerusso@xxxxx.com
> To: vincemcmahon@xxxxx.com
> Sent: Mon, Sep 6, 2021, 8:54 a.m.
>
> Vince,
>
> I recorded footage for a WWE doc this past Friday. It was a great experience; everybody involved was professional and respectful.
>
> I know how busy you are, but I do hope you get the chance to see some of my comments.
>
> I honestly, have no idea what I've ever done. While I'm not looking for a job, all I ever wanted to do was help out in any way I can.
>
> Peace to you and your family.
>
> Vince

Ah, yes—that's how the exchange started; the WWE paid me to be interviewed for some content they were putting out. It was during those sessions that I really opened up about the WWE current product. I wanted Vince to see those comments—that's what started the chain.

OK—I'm trying to put the pieces together here. What might have come next was a text message where I asked Vince straight out if I had any heat with him, or the company, and why. This was his response to that:

> From: vincemcmahon@xxxxx.com
> To: vincerusso@xxxxx.com
> Mon, Sep 6, 2021, 9:19 p.m.

U haven't done anything objectionable at all Vince. Peace to Ur family as well

Started pleasant, so far, right?

WAIT.

From: vincerusso@xxxxx.com
To: vincemcmahon@xxxxx.com
Sent: Tue, Sep 7, 2021, 4:46 a.m.

I am very glad to hear that.

Vince, I'd like to see if I can extend my services to you. We are both getting older and I've just always felt a sense of unfinished business between us. At this point in my life I just want to give back to the fans, the industry, your company, your family and you.

I've been watching *Raw* weekly for over 7 years now. Part of my job as a Professional Podcaster is to observe it, critique it and discuss what I would have done differently. I watch the show from the perspective of a casual fan/television viewer, because that's the perspective in which I always watched it. I look at myself as the masses, and I study—what would the product need to produce to get my viewership on a weekly basis.

I fully believe that in a consultant role I could be of great value to you. I could work directly with you, even if it meant just sending in my thoughts/ideas/insights on a weekly basis. However you think I would be most suitable in adding my 30 years of insight, knowledge and experience to your company and product.

Hope you give it some consideration. I'd love to hear your thoughts.

Clearly you can see I'm interested in a role as a CONSULTANT. I am in no way, shape, or form looking to be a full-time employee. I am extending the offer to help on MY TERMS. I hadn't heard back from Vince, so I followed up a month later as the WWE creative continued to deteriorate.

From: vincerusso@xxxxx.com
To: vincemcmahon@xxxxx.com
Sent: Wed, Oct 13, 2021, 8:43 a.m.

Vince,

Just following up on my last offer to serve you as a consultant. Again, even if you wanted to keep everything confidential between us I would be 100% on board.

I just think I could help you in many ways. For instance, just adjusting the formatting of this past week's show could have helped to make the numbers stronger.

Looking from the outside in, I just believe that I'm able to see things from the television viewer's perspective.

I could also assist you in perhaps sending ideas for talents that may be being underutilized at the moment. I could offer character ideas and story lines.

Vince, I just want to assist you and I know that I still have a lot left in the tank.

If there really is no heat—it's just hard for me to understand why even doing this on a "trial" basis wouldn't be a possibility.

Again, please consider.

Thank you for your time,
Vince

Here's where the text message came.

From: vincerusso@xxxxx.com
To: vincemcmahon@xxxxx.com
Sent: Fri, Oct 15, 2021, 4:19 p.m.

Vince, I just got a text message from *******.

Is this from You?

I just want to confirm. Before I answer.

From: Vince McMahon
To: Vince Russo
Sent: Fri, Oct 15, 2021, 5:42 p.m.

Yes. The only way I'm going to know if U can help us is to offer ideas or critique the show for a couple of weeks. This is not offering U a job; It gives me some idea as potential contributions

Now here's where it starts going off the rails a bit. Remember: I never asked for a job. I wasn't interested in a job. I was looking to consult—to help out on my terms.

From: vincerusso@xxxxx.com
To: vincemcmahon@xxxxx.com
Sent: Fri, Oct 15, 2021, at 5:52 p.m.

Vince,

The success when I worked for you came with the shift of going from Traditional Wrestling to Mirroring Society at the time. Through characters and storylines we made everything we did seem ENTIRELY REALISTIC. That's why casual fans bought into it by the millions. It was a Television show Based in REALITY and they were HOOKED! It had something for EVERYBODY. It was MUST SEE.

WE HAVE COME FULL CIRCLE.

Over the past twenty years—the WWE has once again veered away from that. Today, as a television viewer I'm seeing a straight up wrestling show—really a House Show—and, if I'm not into straight-up, long, continuous wrestling matches—I'm not going to watch the show. It's that simple.

Remember our Pre-tapes? How we would leave the arena? Find unique backstage spots? We made everything look and appear DIFFERENT within our own show. That kept it fresh.

That's why you've experienced a drop in viewership. The only ones watching are the Hard Cores—THEY WILL ALWAYS WATCH—you need to get those Casuals back.

NOTE: I have known Elias since NXT. We established a friendship. He was a fan during the Attitude Era. I have been pitching him ideas for his return—what he has presented to you is the start. A very realistic story that indeed could have taken place.

Vince you trusted me once—it all Begins and Ends with Reality.

That approach will bring the Casuals back slowly—but surely. 100% GUARANTEED. Tony Khan doesn't have a CLUE how to do this. AEW is a Wrestling Company—they will only draw wrestling fans. WWE is a TELEVISION CONGLOMERATE—that has always been the difference—you need to once again DRAW AND WELCOME IN THE MASSES!!!

In formatting—Vince—this week you went to commercial break TWICE promoting two matches that no casual fan would ever care about. You gave the viewer the opportunity to change the channel—and they did. MLB playoffs and Monday Night Football were on. You really need to get back to the STRONG HOOKS going into commercial breaks to assure that you bring the viewers back. These matches—set up with weak hooks—turned them away.

Vince, I've been watching RAW and reviewing it for SEVEN STRAIGHT YEARS.

I know the FORMULA to help bring back the Masses. I knew it then—I know it now.

I will a look at this week's RAW and send you an assessment with some ideas.

Thanks,
Vince

Now, here's where I admit to making a mistake. My knee-jerk reaction was to critique a *Raw* or two like Vince had asked. But then I had second thoughts. Was there really any point to that? Was I just giving Vince an opportunity to dump on my suggestions in an effort to justify to himself that the success of the Attitude Era was all attributed to him, with me having nothing to do with it? Plus—are you telling me that I have to "audition" for a job I didn't even ask for?

Now, it starts getting a little hairy.

From: vincerusso@xxxxx.com
To: vincemcmahon@xxxxx.com
Send: Tue, Oct 19, 2021, 2:29 p.m.

Vince,

I've done a lot of thinking since Friday and I need to be truthful to both myself and you.

Based on our history and the chemistry and success we shared, there's no doubt that I can assist you in various ways with the current RAW numbers. Examples:

- Properly formatting the show which will both ATTRACT and KEEP new viewers weekly
- Developing intriguing, realistic characters that the audience will have emotional ties to
- Plotting out new, fresh, realistic storylines on a weekly basis that will hook the audience and bring them back weekly
- Supplying REAL Dialogue based on how REAL PEOPLE talk . . . Not Just Pro Wrestlers

- Laying out Various Vignettes throughout the show that are different and unique, making each show feel fresh, exciting, new and REAL

Vince, I've made it clear to you, that I am looking to help, but the notion of having to audition in order to give that help . . . is beyond my comprehension. You KNOW what I can do because you saw it first hand for 5 years. You cannot deny the results—they were real.

If you want to compensate me to review RAW for a few weeks—I'll be happy to. But as a professional—with my track record and experience, I can't do that gratis.

I am 60, Vince, with 30 years of experience. I'm not a 22-year-old kid just coming out of college looking for his first break. I want to help. I can help. But, you either want that help . . . or you don't.

We did it before . . . we can do it again.

It's time to get down to work.

Thank you,
Vince

Truthful, Right? Reasonable, yes? Well, that's at least what I thought anyway.

Here it comes.

From: vincemcmahon@xxxxx.com
To: vincerusso@xxxxx.com
Tue, Oct 19, 2021, 6:31 p.m.

That was a long time ago. I have no idea if U can do it now. We're in a PG format. Things and people change. U have a very high opinion of yourself with a ton of failure at WCW. So I retract my offer to show me Ur suggestions for two weeks. If I were U I would have jumped for an opportunity like that. That tells me all I need to know. No need to discuss anymore. I wish U well Vince. Thx for considering

That was it. I never answered Vince's last email. At that point . . . there was no point. Because I wasn't going to jump through hoops in order to help him—he was going to stoop to WCW insults. His ego was hurt. I'm sorry about that, but me trying to *prove myself* to you, when I was just trying to help—just wasn't going to happen.

Was I wrong in my last response to Vince, to not assess the show for a couple of weeks for free? You may think so, but looking back, I don't know: Was I just looking to see if he would admit to needing help simply by getting back to me? Was that my justification? It might have been.

So I left it at that. There was never going to be any more contact with Vince. And I was fine with that.

But I had no idea what was to happen next.

71 THE "ALLEGATIONS"

THIS JUST IN

I have to interrupt the flow of this book for something that just took place a few minutes ago.

I do a lot of freelance work for a company out of India called Sportskeeda. Over the years I have built a solid relationship with them, and there is certainly some mutual respect there.

However . . .

One of the producers there always seems to slip in some "suggested content" that usually revolves around somebody burying me, because he knows it will get a rise out of me. He knows I will then proceed to cut a promo, which he will highlight on their YouTube channel and get clicks galore. I get it—that is the business we're in. Do I appreciate it? No, not at all . . . but I understand dollars and cents.

Well, tonight, this producer played a clip where Eric Bischoff was answering an audience member at one of his "one-man shows" who asked if "Vince Russo ever had any good ideas." Eric took a long pause and said, "Vince Russo has never had one good idea in his entire life."

For starters—think about that. This dude went on an 83-week run of beating the WWF in the ratings. Almost out of a state of desperation, Vince

McMahon hands the reins over to me creatively, and not only is the tide turned, but Eric is eventually sent home packing. So, if the guy who "never had one good idea in his entire life" was partially responsible for your demise . . . what does that say about YOU?

Needless to say, I lost my cool on the show. I lost it because I was upset with the producer for pulling the clip, but to be honest, I was probably more triggered by Eric's smug attitude and same old bullshit.

I would always advise anyone to "take the high road," be "better than that." But when it comes to guys like Cornette and Bischoff, that just hasn't worked. I constantly put those guys over for what they achieved in the business . . . but when it comes to me, neither *ever* have even one kind word to say.

I'm stating all this because this—right here—appeared in the first draft of the book. Now, knowing me, I was going to go back on the second draft and probably edit some of the Eric stuff out. I know I would have said to myself, "Vince, you can't say that!" Guess what? FUCK THAT. I'm not changing a word. I've had it with the Eric Bischoffs of the world. Taking the high road just doesn't work with people like this. They look at your kindness as a weakness, and they use it as an opportunity to prey on you even more. Man, there comes a time when you just have to take the gloves off and stand up for yourself.

NOW is that time.

So, back to those allegations.

"Vince, if you knew who I really was, you wouldn't like me."

Those are the words Vince McMahon spoke to me one day while we were writing TV at his dining room table.

Honestly, at the time Vince said that, I didn't want to know who he really was. That's the reason I always tried to avoid the *inner* inner circle—I never wanted to know what I never needed to know. Whatever Vince was doing behind closed doors—I wanted no part of. But, looking back now, I do somewhat feel like I may have turned a blind eye. There was more to Vince McMahon that I knew about, but those secrets . . . I just didn't care to know.

So, was it a total surprise to me when I learned about Vince and his series of NDAs? Honestly, no. For Vince to have sex with numerous women and then pay them good coin not to tell anybody—that's common business practice when it comes to bosses like Vince McMahon, whether anyone wants to believe it or not. With the money they have, there is a sense that they can buy anything they want—no doubt including sex.

So, yeah, there were some ramifications to those "allegations" that would lead to Vince stepping down from his position as CEO of the WWE; however, apparently, they weren't strong enough as he would soon thereafter regain his seat, even though his own daughter and son-in-law voted against it. A move, I believe, that led to Vince eventually selling the WWE out of spite, so that Stephanie and Triple H could never claim it on his death.

But then, the bombshell dropped—the Janel Grant lawsuit. In this case, not only did a former female employee charge Vince with not making good on one of those NDAs, but she went further—much further—accusing Vince McMahon of SEX TRAFFICKING, claiming that he passed her along to other high-ranking WWE officials. This was now a federal charge, a criminal charge.

The stories that followed were hard to digest, from Vince allegedly sending vile, crass, X-rated, disturbing text messages to Ms. Grant's phone, to him going as far as to allegedly defecating on her head. Man—I can't even believe I just typed that last line.

These explosive allegations forced Vince McMahon to step down *for good*, relinquished of all and any responsibilities he had with the new owners of his company Endeavor. From there, Vince sold all his stock and was apparently done with the wrestling business. Read back that last sentence: Vince McMahon was DONE with the wrestling business.

I never thought I'd see the day. I always envisioned Vince just dropping dead at his desk at the age of 85, 90, somewhere in there. He was never going to give over the reins to the juggernaut of a company he built—never. But now . . . he had no choice. The man had effed up.

Guilty, not guilty, who knows? I am a firm believer in "innocent until proven guilty," and always will be. So, I'll just let this play out with little to no speculation because there isn't anything I know that I'm not sharing with you here. However, inside, I have feelings, emotions, personal things that have been difficult to deal with.

Over the years, in various interviews, I have at times referred to Vince McMahon as a "father figure." I know that many who have worked closely with him over the years have said that. The issue I have, and have always had, is that I don't understand why I feel that way.

When I think of a father figure, I think of my own father. Jim Russo is literally a saint of a man. No, I'm not exaggerating, the man is a SAINT. The kindest, sweetest, gentlest, most loving and caring man you will ever meet. Vince McMahon . . . is none of those things, and the fact is that I thank God that my own father was nothing like Vince. With that said, why would I ever consider him to be a father figure?

Man, this is stifling, conflicting, confusing, something that I just can't wrap my head around. Did those thoughts subliminally come from seeing something different, much different, when I had that alone time with Vince where he let his guard down and allowed himself to just be a "regular" person? Was it that guy who I admired and wished he'd be all the time? For that guy—THAT GUY—was a much different guy. He was blue-collar, one of us, no *bravado*—a term that he loved to use when describing himself. Through that guy you could see a human being who was sincere, honest, scared, and, yes . . . even a victim of his own circumstances.

But unfortunately, it was rare that you would see that version of Vince, and quite frankly . . . you just wouldn't see it enough. You would always see the facade, the boss, the billionaire, the corporate bully, the side that Vince wanted you to see. Man, I feel such a sense of disappointment towards Vince today. I guess that comes from me wanting him to be, and his having the potential to be, a real, caring human being, the one you only saw glimpses of. But that was never going to happen, and it was never going to happen by his choice. He wanted you to believe he was indeed his "Mr. McMahon" character. He wanted you to fear him, feel intimidated by him, and feel less than him. I don't know, maybe that comes with being a billionaire boss, but during the times of my life where I wore my boss hat, I was never like that. I always genuinely cared about people.

In the end, Vince will get what he justly deserves; he is either guilty or he is innocent . . . there is no in-between. My hope? My hope is that justice is served. If Vince is indeed innocent, he should be cleared and exonerated of all charges, and if he's not—Janel Grant should get the vindication that she seeks. It's just sad and unfortunate that it happened.

UPDATE: As of the editing of this book, the potential federal and criminal charges that could have been filed against Vince—weren't. They didn't find enough evidence to continue with their investigation. However, Janel Grant's civil lawsuit is still pending.

72 CLOSE TO THE END

So . . . this is it. This is the end of my trilogy. You will never read another Vince Russo–authored book again. My goal was to always make my story a three-part series, and now I have achieved that. But yet . . . I'm finding difficulty in wrapping this up. I don't know why, but I'm still not feeling a sense of closure when I truly, badly, want one. I just feel like . . . there's more. What that *more* is, I'm not really sure.

There is such a huge part of me that feels guilty because I have zero love for wrestling in my heart. None. So many people ask how can I be so negative about, and frown upon, an industry that gave me an opportunity? My answer—DID IT? Did it actually provide me with an opportunity, or am I still fighting TO THIS DAY to defend myself on a regular basis for basically doing the best job I possibly could when I was a part of the wrestling business? And that's all I did. No matter what job I've had in life, I always wanted to do it to the best of my ability because it ultimately was a reflection of who I was.

And that's what it was all about. That's what it's always been about . . . being the best version of me. The reason I feel the way I do about the business today is on the business . . . not me. It has changed, and none of it for the better. But even though some will say that the business has "evolved," it's not about that, it's about the people covering it and the people supporting it. These people are just not good people. The majority of them are fueled by hate and a sense of entitlement, and, of course—if you're not with them, you're against them. That's what has turned me off of wrestling. Honestly—they can have it.

The industry is at fault in some ways, because they've allowed it. They cater to these individuals. No longer is professional wrestling for everybody, it's now for the "niche"—that hardcore audience with the smallest of presence yet loudest of voices. Those are the people that they listen to. Why? Because it's simply easier to cater to those you already have than to attempt to make new fans. Unfortunately . . . that strategy will catch up with them.

73

MY CABIN IN ESTES

So, as Michael Jackson once labeled what was to be his last tour . . . "THIS IS IT."

I have reached the end of my journey . . . I think. At this point, all I want is my log cabin in the woods. I want to wake up to the fresh mountain air and maybe see some elk on my land.

UPDATE: Amy and I bought the cabin in the woods! However, it wasn't in the Colorado mountains, but rather in Upstate New York. We are currently running it as an Airbnb with the option of perhaps moving there permanently when we both retire.

I want to spend time with Amy; I want to be a good husband. I want to be there for my kids, Will, VJ, and Annie, and give them the utmost love and support that any father can. I want to enjoy my grandchildren, Amelia and Emery, I want them to one day understand who "Papa" REALLY was, and what he stood up for. I want to rub Penelope's belly. I want to give her as many cookies as her heart desires . . . and then just one more.

And, in the end . . . that's what it's all about. That's what it always will be about—your loved ones. The handful of people that you would give your life for, that you love unconditionally, as they do you in return. It's not about fame, money, status, things, or fortune . . . it's about love—true, honest-to-goodness love.

And, in closing, I haven't forgotten you. Those reading this that have been on this journey since day one, those who know me . . . those who understand me . . . those who have accepted me for who I am, what I represent, and the person God created me to be. Thank you for standing by my side through it all. You were the ones who made this great life possible.

I love you.

The end.

74 THEY JUST KEEP PULLIN' ME BACK IN

Since I "finished" writing this, I have appeared on both *NewsNation* and *Piers Morgan Uncensored* twice. I'm currently awaiting a call from a Major Production Company about yet another Vincent Kennedy McMahon/WWE documentary, and THE CLOWNS—aka the Insane Clown Posse (ICP)—are wooing me to go work with them in some talent/creative capacity. It's true—I'm Michael Corleone . . . "Just when I thought I was out . . . they pull me back in!"

Will this always be my life?

Are we looking at a FOURTH INSTALLMENT?

Yeah . . . that is my hook.

I'll see you after the commercial break.

75 BABE RUTH IS DEAD

When I accepted the task of writing this book about 15 months ago, I never imagined it would end this way.

Terry Bollea (Hulk Hogan) is dead.

As I sit at my keyboard just trying to think of the right words to type—a big part of me just can't believe it and still hasn't accepted it. For years and years, the term "The Immortal" Hulk Hogan was used every time he would make an appearance.

Immortal.

I think that, after a while, even I believed that he was. Hulk Hogan *was* Professional Wrestling—PERIOD. Not to diminish the role that others had in the business, Bruno, Dusty, Flair, Austin, Rock, Taker, Sting, Warrior, Foley, etc., but Hulk MADE WRESTLING. He put pro wrestling on the map. He made it "cool," he made it "pop culture." He took it from the carnival stage to over 30 million people watching him and André battle it out on *Saturday Night's Main Event*.

He did that.

Granted, Vince may have given him the platform, but Vince also gave that platform to hundreds, maybe even thousands of others with none of them turning it into the global stage that the Hulkster did. Ruth, Jordan,

Brady, Gretzky, Ali, Woods, Pelé—I put him right up there with those greats, concerning what he did for his sport . . . not to mention Pacino, De Niro, Hoffman, Denzel, and DiCaprio when it came to entertainment. Hulk was *it*. Nobody else came close.

As I'm writing this, it's been seven weeks since Hulk's passing—and since he took his last breath, the industry, the business . . . just doesn't feel the same. And that's simply because it's not. It never will be. We lost the absolute backbone of what professional wrestling both was and should be. Hulk "got it." Perhaps more than any other who ever laced up a pair of boots.

As ridiculous as this may sound to some, I planned on dedicating this book to my two granddaughters, Amelia and Emery, so that they had something to remember Papa by. However, now I'm going to add a third name.

In closing—for real this time—I am dedicating this book to Terry Bollea. Was he the perfect human being? No. Are you? Am I? No. But what he gave to a profession I once loved was HIS LIFE. And by giving it everything he had, and growing the business to the heights that he did, he gave me the opportunity to give my family a good life for the past 34 years. I will forever be indebted to him for that . . . and I will never forget.

Rest in peace, brother—I only wish you knew what you meant to this writer.

God bless.

Entertainment. Writing. Culture.

ECW is a proudly independent, Canadian-owned book publisher. We know great writing can improve people's lives, and we're passionate about sharing original, exciting, and insightful writing across genres.

Thanks for reading along!

We want our books not just to sustain our imaginations, but to help construct a healthier, more just world, and so we've become a certified B Corporation, meaning we meet a high standard of social and environmental responsibility — and we're going to keep aiming higher. We believe books can drive change, but the way we make them can too.

Certified B Corporation

Being a B Corp means that the act of publishing this book should be a force for good — for the planet, for our communities, and for the people that worked to make this book. For example, everyone who worked on this book was paid at least a living wage. You can learn more at the Ontario Living Wage Network.

This book is also available as an eBOUND Digital Certification (EDC) ebook. ECW Press's ebooks are screen reader friendly and are built to meet the needs of those who are unable to read standard print due to blindness, low vision, dyslexia, or a physical disability.

The interior of this book is printed on Sustana EnviroPrint, which is made from 100% recycled fibres and processed chlorine-free.

FSC
www.fsc.org
MIX
Paper | Supporting responsible forestry
FSC® C016245

ECW's office is situated on land that was the traditional territory of many nations including the Wendat, the Anishinaabeg, Haudenosaunee, Chippewa, Métis, and current treaty holders the Mississaugas of the Credit. In the 1880s, the land was developed as part of a growing community around St. Matthew's Anglican and other churches. Starting in the 1950s, our neighbourhood was transformed by immigrants fleeing the Vietnam War and Chinese Canadians dispossessed by the building of Nathan Phillips Square and the subsequent rise in real estate value in other Chinatowns. We are grateful to those who cared for the land before us and are proud to be working amidst this mix of cultures.

ecwpress.com